Everyday People

Also by ALBERT GOLDBARTH

EVERYDAY PEOPLE

Albert Goldbarth

Graywolf Press

This publication is made possible in part by a grant from the Minnesota State Arts Board, through an appropriation by the Minnesota State Legislature from the Minnesota general fund and its arts and cultural heritage fund with money from the vote of the people of Minnesota on November 4, 2008, and a grant from the Wells Fargo Foundation Minnesota. Significant support has also been provided by the National Endowment for the Arts; Target; the McKnight Foundation; and other generous contributions from foundations, corporations, and individuals. To these organizations and individuals we offer our heartfelt thanks.

Published by Graywolf Press
250 Third Avenue North, Suite 600
Minneapolis, Minnesota 55401

www.graywolfpress.org

Published in the United States of America

ISBN 978-1-55597-603-3

2 4 6 8 9 7 5 3 1
First Graywolf Printing, 2012

Library of Congress Control Number: 2011939412

Cover design: Kyle G. Hunter

Cover art: Images from a Japanese syllabary card game

for Skyler,
every day

and in memory of
Marion Stocking
Margaret Rabb

Contents

The Severed Stone Head of Shiva's Wife, and the Bionic Stripper, and Thoreau, and the Cabin Boy in Tahiti, and the Pearl Diver Ravished by Octopi (and Others)

Toward It

What We Were Like (3)

Around us the house sang its evening song: dishes being cleared away, dogs fed, guards settling down for the night watch. I could hear the tread of maids as they went to spread out the bedding, the click of the abacus from the front room as someone did the day's accounts. Gradually the song dwindled to a few constant notes: the deep breathing of the sleeping, occasional snores, once the cry of a man at the moment of physical passion. I found myself thinking of my father, of his longing to live an ordinary human life.

— Lian Hearn, *Across the Nightingale Floor*

I've just finished looking through a book with 16,000 heroes and heroines. Their lives are rather briefly sketched, but the sympathetic reader can guess that there is more romance and tragedy in them than was ever put upon a bookshelf.

— A. T. Burch on a 1920s Topeka, Kansas, telephone book

Most of Us

The starlet and her "intimate device." The aging
Oscar winner raided at his "house of pain."

—We *need* our weekly dose of celebrity scandal,
we whose insides are immeasurably larger

than our skins. We need a second place
to hold the extra "us" of us.

A god can provide it, a mythic hero suffices.
And yet, effective enough for most of us, is

the story of someone else, of *anybody* else, if necessary
of even the neighbors across the street:

because they're *like* you but are *not* you, they're
an isotope of you. The truly interesting halves

of Hercules and Jesus are everyday people.

Everyday People (1)

Everyday People

The oceans are dying. They require a hero,
or a generation of heroes. The oceans are curdling
in on themselves, and on their constituent lives,
they're rising here, and lowering there,
I swear I've heard them gasping. And my friends . . . ?
Are brooding over who their kids are playing with
on the streets. Are coming home after a day where some
midlevel management weasel sucked
their souls out like a yolk from an egg—right through
a tiny puncture-hole in the dome of the skull. The cat
has worms. The price of gas is nearly what
their grandparents' wedding rings cost. The oceans

sorely need a paladin, but my friends are exhausted
disputing how many angels can trample the truth
from a twelve-dollar overcharge on a cell-phone bill.
Our privacy is disappearing, cameras sip it up
like thirsty beasts surrounding a shrinking pool of water, my friends
are worried, oh yes certainly they're worried, but also the tumor
and the marriage and the alcoholic uncle. The war
that's this war but is any war and all war is requesting
a little attention in the cause-part, maybe only
a little more in the effect-part, but my friends know
how impossible it is to attend to even a single other
person sufficiently, plus the dentist, plus the eye exam,
and can't they spend *some* time renewing their sense
of making beauty in this wreckage, Edie
her hummingbird feeders, Sean his libretto, Omar
his amazing organic noodles: something like Balenciaga

the *haute couture* designer whose life I'm reading compulsively
while the ice caps and the red tide and the polar bears,
Balenciaga for whom "the business of making beautiful things
absorbed him totally, and there was no room in his life
for anything else," he did a piece of sewing "every day

of his adult life: from the age of three," in 1913 (age eighteen)
"he was learning the women's-wear trade" as the guns
of the World War cleared their throats and aimed, and through
the world depression, "a fishnet cloak
of knotted white velvet, and swathes of parachute silk
to make pink-and-white flowers," and through
the Spanish Civil War, "regarded making dresses
as a vocation, like the priesthood, and an act of worship,"
through (he bargained with Franco) World War II,
chantilly, chenille, mohair, tulle,
"he took the sample of intractable material
into his sanctum and returned in only moments
with a superbly accomplished buttonhole: it
would have been a half-hour's labor for anyone else,"
a buttonhole while Israel was forged in 1948,
a buttonhole for Sputnik, yes a buttonhole,
a perfect—consummate—buttonhole, is this
a condemnation of my friends (and so myself)

or an exoneration? I truly don't know: any more
than I can tell if the boy in Rembrandt's etching
Christ Preaching (*circa* 1652) is celebrated
or ridiculed (or possibly, with a complicated fondness,
both) for yielding to his innocent daydreams, lost
in drawing figures in the dust on the floor, as only a few
feet overhead, on an impromptu stage in inkily velvet blacks
and the dramatically empty spaces that signify sun,
the Master holds forth with his parables
while a crowd of the commonplace—beggars and burghers—
listen, enrapt. Two-hundred-and-twenty years later,
Adolph von Menzel paints *Departure*
of King Wilhelm I to His Army on 31 July 1870; here
we see the fashionable (and patriotically worked-up) throng,
waistcoated men and richly bustled women by the hundreds

as they line that famous avenue of lime trees, gas lamps,
wind-snapped flags, the Unter den Linden, to witness
their king in his cavalcade, off to join the troops
—at age seventy-three!—in defending their nation
against the French . . . they look at him, these members
of a time and place, as if they form a single compound eye.
Except for the paper boy, with the day's news
over an arm. He has eyes solely for
a friendly dog on the pavement. *Someone* has to
sell the *Berlinsche Nachrichten* (maybe it's
the *Berlinsche Zeitung*). *Someone* needs to carve this
personal moment out of that heavy communal block
of pomp, accomplishment, and (soon, at the battle front)
butchery. This crowd . . . do they disperse,
go home, and that night dream

my dream of my friends? It comes to me so often these days.
My friends who are busily sorting the glass from the plastic
for the recycling cart. My friends the oil change and tune-up,
the interview, the team to cheer, the argument
and the apology—and some of them the intricate and cheesy
psychological architecture (like the windmill-strewn
and dragon-populated Putt-Putt golf course) of denial
of the need for an apology. My friends the e-mail list
on carbon footprints. And a tad of porn. With guilt,
with beer, with in-laws, with the lawn, with the tuition.
With their lo-cal, and their hi-tech, and deluxe.
I see them gathered, and then falling
down a long and floating drop, not
through an astronomer's darling black hole, not
through Alice's Wonderland rabbit hole, but

falling through a buttonhole,
into the lives of everyday people.

Natural State

I'm sitting at Nathan's, reading a biography of Darwin
who, right now, is dissecting a barnacle

"no bigger than a pinhead (and with two penises)":
he'll work like this on barnacles, his wrists supported

by rigged-up blocks of workshop wood, for eight years.
Nathan is reading too, in the worn-down banged-up "daddy chair":

those philosophical poems of William Bronk's. What's
most delightful is that Tristan, 11, and Aidan, 10,

are reading, each of them enmazed in a fantasy novel
that squeezes them by the attention-bone behind the eyes

in its thimble pool of pineal juice and drizzled endorphins.
Tristan cared enough to cry when he finished his previous book

and its battle of shadow and radiance was over.
Each of us: his individual book; and yet

the silence is communal. This is a natural state
at Nathan's. Rebecca, however, is reading the Sunday paper

and so serves, without saying a word, to remind us
how natural it was for Raeshawn Nelson, 7,

to fall while running and burn out his eye
on the disregarded meth pipe, or for Anna Rietta, 9,

to have come home from school and excitedly been
the **!star!**, each day, of the homemade porn her parents

peddled as "young fun" over the internet. This
was what they knew, and all they knew, and so they entered it

as comfortably as Tristan does his opened world
of sorcerors and valiant knights and fancy-talking beasts, since use

x frequency = familiarity. That's the strict, imperious math
of *everybody's* insular subuniverse. Sherena asked me what

this thing "vermouth" was (she pronounced it "mouth") and ordered
quiche as if it were the brother of "touché"; but then

she needed to explain to me why C-C was the "bottom bitch"
and what a "T-girl" is and how to put down money

on Ice's book at "the county," by which
she meant jail. And those years when Darwin parsed

the slimy fiber of his barnacles (discovering the species
where "the female has no anus" and the one with "tiny parasitic

males [that were] embedded in one female's flesh like blackheads"),
"squinty . . . laborious," were among the final decades of hundreds of years

when a woman in China would suffer ritual footbinding,
at five, the bandages limiting growth until the toes

were bent and curled (the toenails growing into the balls of the feet)
and the arches broken. This resulted in the desirable

"shrunken plums" and "three-inch golden lilies" sought
by marriage brokers. Traditionally, a prospective mother-in-law

would check below the hem, and reject any feet
over four inches long. Entire generations of women could only

mince and hobble. And this was natural, this was the air
and the light and "the-way-of-things-forever" that

you woke up into every day . . . as natural as the implicit laws
in Aidan's book, by which a bear converses

with a girl in growly mutualspeak, and a boy
of sturdy heart and his wingéd horse ascend

their sky with the unremarkable grace of birds
in ours. That's ordinary Newtonian physics there, and Aidan

subjects himself to the rules of flying horsemanship,
and the code of those of innocent spirit

about to war with wyverns and the wormfolk, and
the governing instruction of gods with the heads

of wide-eyed animals . . . and even now, Sherena texts
my phone to say that WEATHER GOOD and SHINE

GOT BULLET IN LUNG FROM POLICE, as if
these two reports were equally weighted. There's

that famous and charming anecdote in which Darwin's
second son George is at the house of a playfriend,

looking around, and casually asks him
"Where does *your* father do his barnacles?"

Our Heroine Ellen, and Three Pals

Alia Sabu, 18, is "the world's youngest college professor."
Check. The eruption of Mt. Vesuvius occurred in 79 AD,
and victims left hollows that "cast in plaster, yield details
as eerily fine as the imprints of one man's eyebrows." *Check.*
Over in England, Guy Hawkes Day is celebrated
Whoa. Fawkes. Check. If Keats had had
a publisher's fact-checker overpresiding his own
pell-mell exquisitudes, the European discovery
of the Pacific would never have been—as it was,
and as it remains—misattributed. Ellen ticks
mechanically down the list that will lead her to lunch
(with Thelma the poetess, Short George king
of the online crypto-universe, and Dora the orphan
and amateur genealogist: her fact-checker pals), so one

two three, it's: *distance of Epsilon Eridani; name*
of the Japanese lunar orbiter; date of the earliest
temple so far excavated . . . and all the while the "her"
of her, the irreducible I, is floatingfloating,
like a dust mote, like an astronaut untethered,
through the fancies the subconscious burbles fecundly
nonstop in us . . . in her, right now, a sea-breeze beach
beyond the blot the X-ray hunted down in her shoulder,
beyond the divorce . . . she floats . . . there is no fiction-checker
hired by the brain, in fact the brain *requires* a space
in itself ungoverned by the actual . . . the moon
in the waves, the scent of the lei of flowers that serves
to complement her neck and naked breasts . . . *10.5 light years;*

Kaguya; 10,000 BC. The joke at lunch is
they yell "check!" at the flustered waiter in unison.
Short George tells Thelma he could build an online crypto-England
in which Keats survived and married Fannie Brown, *no,*
Fanny Brawne, *check.* They all riff on this delightful possibility
a little ("Twins." *Twins?* "Pair o'Keats."), with Dora

all the while, all this same time, also sitting in the cellar
of her mind and in its private dark imagining
the kiosks and the poverty and the bright flags in the springtime
in those two East European countries she knows her parents
came from though she doesn't yet know which . . . the woman
about to be her mother making clumsy girlish vamp-eyes
(over the suds of the backyard laundry tub) at the man,
the private in spit-shine boots and dapper mufti, about

to become her father, as these two *(now*
the various fantasies blend in one communal psychic weather)
parakeets coo on a swing in their gilt-work bird cage
in a parlor where the Keatses are—the phone rings,
"John would you please answer / *phone?* / [well, yes,
a retropostulated steampunk phone they call
a transaudion] the trans?"—"Hullo? Keats
residence." "Hello, sir, my name is Alia Sabu. I'm
an assistant professor of English engaged in researching
your sonnet on Chapman's Ovid *(no)* on Chapman's Homer
(check) and"—then the frying-pan noises and sputtering out
of global communications as the smutch from Vesuvius
circles the earth—"Fanny!" "John, the children!"—the plume of it
so high even Kaguya is floatingfloating like a fishing bob

riding a current—"The children are drowning . . . !"—and work
resumes. Our heroine, Ellen, is back
at her task of verification . . . even as, somewhere inside her
no less needed and persuasive than the place
of her employment (and its mission to confirm), she
heeds those cries, she rises immediately from her languor
on the sands, she races pell-mell to the violent waves
—her lei is lost to the evening air—and pulls the two
Keats children from their near death in those crazily
volcano-flustered waters. . . . Jacob Pinker-Sachs: "No matter

how coolly rational the small globe of our consciousness is,
it rides on a heated sea of childlike play;
and alternative selves and trial-and-error futures
nod and wobble on the top of this like fishing bobs." (I made

that up.) At home tonight Short George is making up,
online, the rules and shoes and musics and peninsulas
of an entire cosmos. Why not? Someone hurt him
once, and here he heals. Someone grabbed him
by the smitten-bone, grabbed him by the spigot
where the juice of infatuation enters the blood, and he was severely
pummeled, and never the same, but here he's the master
of clouds and swords and fishing fleets and mass migrations
and here he can sorcer into existence a cure for the thing
that eats its way through Ellen's shoulder and Keats's lungs,
and here Short George can manfully declare his love for Dora,
which he'd never do in the bruises and blades of the "real world,"
and Dora right now is online finally nailing down
her parents' nationalities. Hungarian. Czech.

"The Human Condition"

—of course. What *else* is there to write about?
Somewhere this side of the smelting-fires,
the sabers are being forged; and kingly broadswords,
in a shower of sparks; and those wicked, twisty
dagger blades the hillmen use; there is, after all,
such devil-spawn apostasy to fight against: the tents
to torch, the villages to turn to kindling.
Somewhere else, another kind—a metaphoric kind—
of conflagration fills the flesh: entire dynasties,
and courts of law, and mothers' sleep, will sunder
and snap like fat on the grill, as lust consumes
its way across the borders of two young people's lives,
the way lust will, the way that joy
in our sexual selves is zealous for completion . . .
just as somewhere else, it's the sudden combustion
of godly light in a penitent's breast that carries
in it the vision of warrior seraphs
and a grace so intense that it sears. . . .
Worlds shake. There is gnashing, there are hosannas.
Even so, if the "condition" is "human,"
it also must attend
                              to Neil
losing at online poker tonight. And Chandra:
totaling her acceptance and rejection slips.
And Juddie Q: his regular connection,
who he trusted, delivered a bag of product
obviously cut with inferior goods from someone else's
dead-end hustle. And Della: rosining
her bow; and thinking soon her chin
will be cupped—we might say intimately
cupped—and the strings will take her away
on their boulevard into another world. And Dan:
a week of committee meetings. Little things;
little things. My grandparents
                              came here

from Russia and Poland over a century back now.
Orthodox Jews are supposed to avoid all secular labor
over the Sabbath—cooking, for instance, or even simply
striking a light. And so one burner on the stove
might be left on, at a minimum level, the way
that earlier an ember might be saved
for as long as possible through the night
—kept low, and patient
in case a greater flame was called for.

The Poem of the Little House at the Corner
of Misapprehension and Marvel

" . . . during Napoleon III's coup d'etat when one of his
officers, on being informed that a mob was approaching
the Imperial Guard, coughed and exclaimed, with his
hand across his throat, *'Ma sacree toux!* (My damned
cough).' But his lieutenant, understanding him to say
'Massacrez tous! (massacre them all!),' gave the order to
fire, killing thousands—needlessly."

— Guy Murchie

"He was mortared to death."
A pity, how we misspeak and mishear.

—Or "martyred"? Not that /coin-flip/ either
makes a difference to the increasingly cooler

downtick of a corpse's cells. "We heard the crazy mating joy
of the loon across the water." Yes, but what

do *we* know, amateurs that we are? Loon, shmoon.
It might have been dying, announcing

its pain in those trilling pennants. It might
have been the girl who was lost in these woods last week

and never found by the volunteer searchers,
it might have been her ghost

with an admonishment. The truth is,
even among ourselves we often can't distinguish pain

from pleasure, not in our beds, our hearts, the tone
of a poem on the final exam (a coin-toss). A pity, because

we know the urgency of some utterance;
and the intended goodwill of our listening; and

the marvelous basic mechanics of speech,
of lung: 300 million alveoli that, "if spread out flat,"

as my eighth-grade science teacher preened, "would come to
750 square feet, the entire floor space of an average house,"

and she added that tired magic about how atoms
of Julius Caesar and Napoleon and Beethoven did

their fleet anachronistic dance in every inhalation
of ours, although at thirteen I preferred to think

that the atoms of Cleopatra's body—*my* Cleopatra,
inflating her see-through empresswear

with husky breaths—commingled with my blood, and also
realized in my own dim way it wasn't only Einstein,

Shakespeare, Madame Curie populating my oxygen,
but also the smelly and scabby old man

from across the street who'd died last year
when the late-shift ward nurse heard (as she said in her testimony)

"med injection" instead of (as the outgoing
ward nurse told her) "bed inspection"—altogether

an unfortunate example of my theme . . . although
exempla abound, misapprehension

also dancing inside us at the atomic level.
Someone thought the gate was locked, she *always* locked

the gate in the late afternoon when the haze set down
and the sun for a moment seemed to caramelize the lake top,

so the gate was locked; except that it wasn't,
and seven days into it nobody's found the girl

or a scraggle of hair or a single ribbon. I tell you
we're amateurs, we're sometimes bungling amateurs,

of the minutiae of our own lives. When I heard the sounds
that gurgled from my chest as my wife was leaving

into the dense, conspiratorial Austin, Texas night,
I couldn't have said if it was defeat

or relief. She couldn't have said which one
she'd have been happiest to cause. We only knew

that I'd been wrong at times, and she'd been wrong at times,
and that our total errors, if spread out flat,

become the house we live in. They're another system
inside us, along with the cardiac and the pulmonary,

they're moving us toward the horizon line. And when
enough errors accumulate there, that's what

we call the future. Even now, as you read this,
someone in that unknowable distance

is breathing you in.

Miles

American produce travels an average of nearly fifteen
hundred miles before we eat it.
                        — Michael Specter, in the *New Yorker*

The Anderschorns were the first of our neighbors to get
an RV, and from that day on we saw them only
at Christmastimes. "They travel around the year!"
my mother said with a kind of wonder
in her voice, as if they'd snapped the chains
of ordinary living. That may picture her
as quaint, naive—I suppose she was, in a way—
but there *is* a magical fascination
accruing to mileage. Many thousands
for the migratory circuits of some birds, and yet
those star charts fit in brains that fit
in walnut (or pistachio) shells. The salmon drags across
the final miles of migration and it dwindles
in its task, like an eraser. The miles
of Marco Polo, Lewis and Clark, the space repairmen
rocketed up to tune the Hubble telescope.
And distance is tricky, it has its strange compactions
and its cattywampus jumps: a few vertical yards
of certain shale will take us from Pez-and-cell-phone
here-and-now to the tank-tread wriggle-life
of the Devonian. A particle of comet dust
"one-millionth of an inch wide" looks like any dust,
but this one in the photo holds the one-and-only sample
we have of a mineral called brownleeite
and was captured "by an ER-2 high-altitude plane
in the stratosphere, which begins about eight
miles up." Not that the waft of dust
my parents have become is less astounding for its origin
nearby and underfoot. My mother poured me
local apple juice where chill and sweet were brilliantly

indistinguishable, but that was 1954; today, and off
the supermarket shelf, it comes from China,
which in apple years is comet rings away.
American produce . . . ! It will bear the dung and the sand-shear
of the caravan, it will materialize from a lengthy blur
of speed like a cartoon mouse, it will delight us
with its stories of the Khan and the roc
and a Buddha the height of a granary, it will leave a trail
of carbon uselessly burning behind it
until we eat it, and more of it, and burn
ourselves and the planet.

• •

There was a tree—a standard dispirited
but sufficient Chicago curbside tree—outside
the curtained window of my father's hospital room
when he was diagnosed, and I remember
its greenery as a counterpoint to the gray of his face
and the gray of the telltale X-ray,
just as I remember the perfect ice
that clarified each twig of it
when he returned to die there.
Though I've never climbed the Pyrenees
or gondola'd in Venice
I can tell you this about travel:
Our death is born in the cells of us.

when we take a step
it takes a step

• •

Holiday gifts from the Anderschorns became no more
than souvenirs of their life on the road—a Statue of Liberty

ashtray, or a toothpick dispenser cleverly enough
designed like a redwood—but these knickknacks were dispensed
and accepted with ceremony (and, given our own more
sedentary days, with awe) you'd think would attach
to the public unveiling of ancient Egyptian artifacts
—a casket mask of gold, an exotic scorpion goddess
figured out of cedar and lapis lazuli—untombed
from some multimillennial dark and given now,
in the civil light of a museum, to the inspection
of scholars and dignitaries. Best of all
was marveling at their maps—"and we were here,
and here, and here"—that proved to us the unknown
could be mastered by these good, straight people
rulering the good, straight lines from A to B.
And distance is tricky—not all of it yields
readily to our gauges and itemized lists.
At death the *ba* and the *ka*—depicted in the scrolls
and on the walls as human-headed birds—are released
from the quieted chest. At death
the real travel starts: the Boat of Ra is rowed
through the night-and-the-sky-that-are-One, and then
you enter the Hall of Justice and weigh your heart
against the Feather of Truth, and then you pass through the gates
called Accurate Plumb-Bob, Mother-Toe, Offering-Wine, and Ox of Geb,
and through the Twelve Districts of Night, and then into
the Fields of Reeds, on and on, for eternity. . . .
All of that, out of this mummified package.

the body is here
but its person is journeying

• •

Distance is slippery.
One of its tricks: it masquerades

as time. How far have I pilgrimaged
since 1954, when I was six,
and I was good and straight and rulered,
and I pledged the flag, indeed the entire
world, with a trust in the system
of exporting copper, importing bananas, celebrating
local saints and navigators
in wooden shoes or turbans or serapes. . . .
How many wars ago. How many books about the CIA
ago. How many jolly apples that cost misery
to arrive here, every bite I take of every 1,500 miles
eating a hole in the air. We didn't know when I was six

what her smoking would do to her, but of course
it grimed my mother's lungs to uselessness.
She's smiling, though, in the photograph
from 1954, she's blithely finger-tapping an ash
to a growing pile of ashes that, thanks to the Anderschorns,
are heaped here, and continue to heap,
at the feet of the Statue of Liberty.

• •

The miles in the prime filet.
The miles in the plum, in the turbot, in the caramel filling.
Phew!—my hair was fast, it raced
to get this gray. The miles of nerve
if they were unbundled out of the body,
and the traffic they bear. A wildebeest
is how many miles? A hummingbird is how many miles?
The long trek from the ovum to the grave.
I once said something to a woman I knew
that traveled through the death scenes of the *Iliad*
before it left my lips. The Large Hadron Collider

smashes protons in the hope of "recreating conditions
that last occurred a trillionth of a second
after the Big Bang"—not that Arnie's second marriage
wasn't also a way of recreating, of traveling to,
the past. The walk from cellblock
to electric chair, "the last mile," might seem quicker
than the 186,324 miles light zips through
in a second. Although for us—our human eyes—that
isn't "travel," it's "instantaneity." I once did something
disreputable and I once did something honorable
and they were hobos, tramping the roads for weeks,
were twins in every way, before they left my heart.
Before my mother died, the scraggly Chicago catalpa
in our front yard circled completely from flowering pod
to emburdening snow, then back.
The clock hands: how many miles?

a tree is rooted but travels
around the year

What We Were Like (1)

How Did They Live?

We itch to know
        the girl
who held this svelte bone sewing-needle
from 15,000 years back—an "artifact" (*we* say)
packed in the earth
like a bone in a herring, and just now
fished up into the light.
          And the girl?—we
need to see her asleep in her animal skins, or
flensing-out tenacious layers of fat
from half-done sleeping skins, or humming over the rendering
of fat to its dozenfold uses. Is she humming
a "tune"? Does she carry a "name"? We need to know
the whole compacted mosaic of food in her bowel
as well as the gods in her heart. In
an "artist's rendition," gray smoke from a cavemouth fire
unwinds a log in long wafts,
slubbing the air. Around this center, the Neanderthal
inhabitants of Shanidar Cave—their scrapers,
choppers, gougers, set aside for now—attend a formal
burial, bringing sprays of woody-horsetail,
cornflowers, yarrow, hollyhock, ragwort: parts of some
arrangement time has since dissolved.
We lust to thumb the nub
of *their* lust's version of pillow talk
and its politics. . . .

      • •

We want the lip of the ewer, the rib of the corset,
the intimate fit of quotidian minutiae.
          In this
photograph from 1913, six men hold the body of a snake,
and still its angular head and muscular comma of tail

dangle laxly off the ends of that line of support. The thump
by which our hearts react to high adventure and exoticism
goes adrenalin-crazy at this—but once
it calms, the more abiding wondering
takes over: how did they keep their fires
in tropical rains, what foodstuffs
in their tins, whose faces in cameo
in their lockets?
                              Wars are wars, but
what *shitte-stoole* the regent sat upon while fulminating,
its silk and its octagon nailheads . . . ah!
                                                        One January
a tire blew out. I skidded, then stopped, below a sky
the color of battleship plating; there wasn't one
degree around to goose the mercury. In minutes,
half the block was out there, offering advice, "go easy
on the jack," "stand this way for leverage," "grip the lug-nuts
so," amazingly eager to excavate and polish
the small earned wisdoms of their lives, to join
in this 21st-century urban tableau, to lend me
velcro-wristed gloves and a thermos of coffee,
tribal for a moment, sure of the ritual,
weaving recognized pattern into their day,
and all of their days, contributing breath
to a great white anaconda in the air.

A Story

I call it a "walk poem." You
know, "I saw this; I saw this."
— Margaret Rabb

And then the gunk was gently but forcibly
washed out from my eyes. The circumcision:
they sedated me the traditional way, a handkerchief
was twisted into a suckable teat and then dipped
into wine. I remember, even in first grade, being
enamored of certain girls who jounced a certain
something into their sway. I call it
the life poem: you know, first this happened and then
this happened too. We write so little
about the gods anymore—when was the last time Zeus
assumed an animal form in a poem (or glowered
the heavens themselves into a mimetic frown)
with serious depiction —and even history
has been snipped away from our ongoing voom
as if it were just a placenta we didn't need
to feed on any longer, and now it's all
the serial this and this and this that happens
to that person in your bedroom mirror: I graduated,
I did a year (with two weeks in the hole)
for possession, I fucked, I triumphed, I *got* fucked . . .
for without these linear discs we'd have
no spine; without a spine, no electrical zip
between the brain and its lovely and painful
and fraught and marred and lumped and sweetcream fleshly baggage.
In terms of the art, this recent delimiting
of vision to our autobiographical selves is,
maybe, a diminishment. I bore the child,
I tarred the roof, I ai-yi-yi. And yet a walk
around Olympus must have come down to the narrative
and the quotidian too: the council of gods convened;

the lightning clinked inside its cloud like coins
in a pouch that were eager for spending; fire
came to exist, then sex, then war, then this
and this, the pinions of a swan,
the usual love-fests and betrayals. Even history
implies sequential happenstance—a story—although
we "know" this is in part our human need to read causation
into our serendipity-finds of homo erectus bones,
and the backroom plotting of timber and oil barons,
and the marriages and sunderings that mark dynastic lines
like the knots on a quipu, "I walked through the rubble
and glitz of the latter twentieth century, and I saw X,
which was flabbergastingly horrid, then Y, then Z,
these left me beaming out a living light
like an angel pricked with breathing holes." And
in January earlier this year, on my sixty-first birthday,
I went for a walk below the dirty gray
meringue of the sky. The rock salt
strewn the night before had already made a lace
of the ice sheen on the sidewalk. There were trees
on one block hosting crows to a volume, an opacity,
that their leaves could never have matched. Two boys
of five or six were blimping around in snowsuits
as if practicing for a spacewalk. In the corner
taco joint, a couple sharing a sodden monterey
held hands across the booth, and the gloves they'd removed
and placed on their table duplicated that tender gesture.
On the TV screen, a little girl in a shroud
(about the size of the torah they carry held to their chests
around the synagogue at the Sabbath service)
was set in a crate, and there was weeping enough,
and raised-fist vows of violent reprisal enough,
to make the stones of the desert moan in pity.
I saw this. I saw this.

The Winds

In those days I desired love, or what
I took for love—but I was helpless,
I required chance to get me there,

I thought of pollen: powerful,
but needy of breeze
or the belly-furze of a bee.

· ·

The job that bore some friends from Oregon
to a cypress-kneed and alligator-infested
town in Louisiana. The compound possibilities

for sexual pairing in any given community.
These are the winds. The winds that carry
our DNA through the air like milkweed.

· ·

In a painting the people on either side of the boulevard
are large and excited and various and full of that
exuberance we call everyday life: but smaller

yet approaching is the armor glint of marching troops
as silver as sardines, in a current that's bringing
some change to all of these lives, and even to styles of painting:

· ·

is what I said in the bar, intent on sounding
irresistibly knowing. To some I was geeky;
to some, oh-please-shut-up. But lovely others found me

a dessert for the night worth circling around, and there
were smoky snakes of alt-rock music, and magnetic fields
of spritzy perfume, and undulant laughter, and all of it

• •

lifted the little seeds we were on the big
transgenerational tides: a glitter of genome on the wind,
a tangle of pheromones on the wind,

short atoms of longing.

STD

And SDS: "Students for a Democratic Society," that
radical-hippie-protest-movement youth group

of the 1960s. When I was a junior in high school
my parents were "worried sick" those "college punks"

would taint me, just one evening of their politics,
a word, a wink, would be a roaring pipeline

of corruption. Although really I only wanted to be there
flirting around with Lena Greenberg—*that* was body politic

enough for me, at sixteen. And indeed it only took
a wink, a microscopic jot . . . and then

the rash, and the frightening urinary fire,
and the doctor's swab he said would be "uncomfortable"

and agonied like a bullet up my penis shaft.

• •

Whatever part of the earth is in the sky
connives to return—and so it rains;

and so it snows; and so the locusts settle
eventually with such a hunger for earth,

it disappears in them before they fly again.
And the gods . . . they also settle,

briefly, here on our level; and they also have hungers,
ask Adonis or Leda: we're the custards

of an evening, for the gods, and whatever off-the-scale
invisible spirochete of wham-bam otherworld exposure

is involved, its consequences are measured by dynasties
arising or toppling, countrysides redistricted, and people

metamorphosed into marble, flower, bark, wind,
and transanimal bodies of every conceivable species.

It's like lightning: it might only take a contact-point
on the skin the size of a dime or less, the size

of a needle tatting your lover's initials into your ass
or less, and yet you could be lifted and flung

a quarter-mile into the neighbors' milo.
All of the oldest stories—ancient Athens, Bethlehem, etc.—

somewhere in them feature a person who implores the sky
to come down with its majesty. It only requires

a hair to be touched, one pore, and the story ends
in a dazzle of glory. (Or a pile of ash.)

• •

Somewhat to my current shame, I've never been arrested
at a protest march. But I know what I think;

and I know how I vote; and I know what I'd do
if the power were mine. It turns out that my parents

were right, that forty-years-or-more ago. Its symptoms
didn't bloom in a week like Lena-love; but neither

are they curable, I'm happy to report
—these strong convictions from those early opened eyes.

Ws

It wasn't someone puffing a monster doobie, it
was Zito's van's exhaust in the lilac evening air, but
this was 1971 and thus that metaphoric capability
came easily, the joint was passed, the congregants
on Noni's porch were . . . "stoners" I guess is the word,
although Emilio was a journalism major too and an aspirant
toward a night in Amy's army surplus pants, and
Noni was also a single mother of two and a stripper
out at Tyme 4 Fun, and Zito studied philosophy when
he wasn't under that van with a wrench and a hundred
curses yelled forth like ball lightning, he
was also the son of a woman who ran for Congress
with a pro-war plank her party nailed mightily into her platform,
which conflicted his pacifist soul, for 1971 was not
the year of marijuana only, but also the year the war
was levering friends and family apart, and also
the year that Zito's mother had the lump checked out
in a room where the wattage turned her into a frozen doe
in headlights (this had happened once
to her son, and explained the canted fender that always
gave his van the look of having suffered a stroke) and she
walked into the night with her medical news
around her like a necklace with a living bird
between her breasts for a pendant, and it kept trying
to fly, to lift her off the earth and toward the little
crib death spaces in between the stars, so empty
and so sad, because the earth was also a vector of time
and space that traveled implacably through
the universe, and took us with it so fast
we were a cloud (said Amy, exhaling a particularly
emphatic one herself) and Emilio started to explain
the staunch five Ws of journalism, but who
and what and when and where and why, he said, were
dead in the twentieth century, and then he shrugged,
so tenderly, with a gesture that took in all of us.

Minnows, Darters, Sturgeon

That there's a *fun* in *funeral*
is goofus etymology, but a sensible reminder
of the secret life in everything . . . how inside *dear*
is *deer* and, inside that,
the Sanskrit: "falls to dust and perishes."
If we could hold a word
against our ear, like a shell,
we'd hear its sea—churning in its belly,
the size of blood in a mosquito.

The way inside us is
the genome's part of its ongoing
conversation with the universe.
The way the ageless story of the seed is still
inside the Nile reed; and the song
of the reed, inside the sheet of papyrus
—under the tallies of sweet downriver wheat
and chariot wheels and waxy cones of floral perfume:
another language.

The hos, the speeders, and the married slappers
never stop, they pile up like autumn leaves,
but under the scurf of the forest preserve
the "cold case" is muttering patiently, and waiting
the creation of technology that will finally point
a revelatory finger. Forgetting is only remembering
thinned with foreign particles.
If the Neolithic village is ever excavated
out of its silencing earth, the wind
will still know the notes. One night
the woman lightly places her fingertips
on the head of the man asleep beside her:

somewhere hundreds of brain-equivalent miles down
inside him is a database
of fossils of earlier women. Later,

his turn: with his ear against her back,
between the shoulders: there, the whole script
of an alternate reality is being recited (someone
plays his part) in a drama
compounded of glial cells and electrical links.
Today I heard the radio interview
of someone who studies the sounds fish make;
her special focus is minnows, darters, sturgeon.
They're noisy, it turns out, when you have
the proper equipment . . . thundering booms
and drawn-out kiss-squeak figure prominently
in these fierce displays of territoriality
and sexual welcome underneath
the still and quiet surface.

Bone

One reason for our pleasure
in the sexual parts—the rich spill
of the breasts, the many-personalitied
cock, the slippery ingress
and its complicated fragrance—is they let us forget,
as much of us won't, that there's a skeleton
inside, waiting, just like the one
that hung from the hook in science class
and clattered when a ruler counted
implacably down the ribs.

· ·

In this shadowy fifteenth-century engraving,
the skeleton sits at a table, chin on fist,
quill pen in its other hand
—five centuries before Röntgen's invention.
Somehow, although it's hard to believe,
the semen already has this solid structure
promised inside it. And a nipple
is porous so beautifully . . .
a delivery system for calcium.

· ·

Massaging her back: the feel
in her shoulders of that scapular unyielding,
below the doughy pliancy of muscle.
I suppose I could think it morbid, and yet
my thumbs along the bump-trail
of the spine are pleased to travel by touch,
blunt and eyeless things that they are.
If sound waves have a consciousness,
then sonar might delight like this
when it strokes a ridge under the ocean.

October

Another poem struck into being by seeing
a vee of geese overhead, a wing-shape

that's composed of its several dozen element-wings
on loan to the greater body. This becomes an argument

(of isolation versus community) given immediate,
visible form; a stream is taking the mountain

away, but at a pace we'll never see—unlike
this sky-adorning passage timed

by mere coincidence to human comprehension.
And we learn, by the absorption of these single, scattered creatures

into one majestic pattern, how a proper use
of "beauty" is in service

to "beatitude"—the rising of a concept
into something more, some larger, further order

of existence. I suspect I'm not
the only one who's stood here with the groceries leaking

out of the paper bag, and the volts that bump in the heart
like small trapped minnows of longing, and our evanescence

burning in the way that a leaf is green flame
on its ordained path to orange—here, defined

by "the futility of work in the face of destruction"
(the phrase is Rachel Cohen's)—and looked up

to imagine he belonged with them, but
was abandoned, missed the call

to gather and to lift as one, so now
can only stare at their increasing distance,

maybe in the way that, once, the Lost Tribes
looked to see the rest of Israel

continue warring and praying and sowing
and loving by starlight

into the future without them.

Coming Back

Chinese grandmother Jin Guangying, 77, from the town of
Shuyang in Jiangsu province, suffered crippling headaches and
went to visit a doctor. An X-ray revealed a rusting 64-year-old
bullet in her brain. / Doctors in Hanoi have removed a bullet
from the heart of a Vietnamese soldier 39 years after he was shot
by U.S. troops in the Vietnam War. / An Australian had a bullet
removed from his lower left lung 56 years after he was shot by a
Japanese machine-gunner during World War II.

– compiled from Fortean Times

Not that I'd elect to step in front of one—but
obviously these little Trojan horses of death
are overrated. Disappearance itself is disappointing,
if we look to it for 100 percent success.
In 1867, in India's Sutlej Valley, a single bird
was discovered, so distinct that it became what science calls
the "type specimen" of a new species: large-billed
(anyway, large for its body length) reed warbler.
Then it vanished. None was seen again. Its song,
its fussy ruffle, its viscera . . . vanished; evolutionary
dew. Until, that is, the 27th
of March, 2006, "when one was captured alive
in a wastewater treatment center outside of Bangkok"
—picked (again) from the darkness as if by a lighthouse beam
that completes its rotation every 139 years.
Old Faithful. . . . Halley's Comet. . . . These seem marvelous
because of their infrequency—and not because of their principle,
the ho-hum same as the sun's, the moon's.
If Rupert Sheldrake's theory is correct,*

---

* "Memory is inherent in nature. . . . Natural systems, such as termite colonies, or pigeons, or orchid plants, or
insulin molecules, inherit a collective memory from all previous things of their kind, however far away they
were and however long ago they existed." This is true for humans as well. "Our memories may not be stored
inside our brains," but in "fields, called morphic fields," which are "non-material regions of influence extending
in space and continuing in time. . . . Morphic fields do not disappear: they are potential organizing patterns of
influence, and can appear again physically in other times and places." (Sheldrake, *The Presence of the Past*)

there is no absolute oblivion: a sort of sea of pre-
and post-existingness surrounds us. In *The Land
of the Lost,* a 1950s children's radio program,
Jack and Judy visit the realm of the supposedly irretrievable
—missing buttons, keys, etc.—and adventure there,
renewing their acquaintance with these old
familiar objects. Not that we should take an easy
consolation from such moments. The passenger pigeon isn't
going to pull the Lazarus act, the famous
phoenix 360°, of that reed warbler: not a one
of the dozens of miles of thundering clouds of those birds
survived our sharp and profligate aim;
nor will my mother ever boil water for the tea
again, or nightly wipe the dog's eyes of their rheum,
or light her husband's *yahrtzeit* candle
when his death-day circles back: that candle flicker
and that kettle steam remain here
on the planet, but not her. Still, there are stories: someone's
hearing or sight is said to return,
a decade later; someone's wallet, wedding ring,
in a shark, in a copious shepherd's pie, in a cow poop,
in the gorgeous and violent disbursal of a tornado
—and somebody mails it back. Our childhoods *never*
disappear completely, and their whinings, fears
and wonders only hibernate, a bonsai of us, *in* us,
the way the first ring of the redwood is still
at its center, inside the enormity. The poet Gregory Orr
—and he's an exceptional talent—accidentally
shot his older brother Peter to death
when he was twelve, one day in the lightening gray
of a deer-hunt dawn in the Hudson Valley
almost fifty years ago. And every poem he's written
is that bullet coming back.

An Explanation

I wanted to say
          that everything was difficult, the moon was required
to crawl first with its elbows then its knees
across the sill of the window before it could enter my room
and, when it did, when it stood there releasing its light
like any two-cent break-and-enterer's sweep across the objects
there, creating them like stupid startled sheep from out
of darkness, when that happened and I saw how insufficient were
my days and nights and bricabrac, then the taste of regret
infused my tongue—a sour taste, a small toy taste,
it can't stand like a huge stone Babylonian
temple griffin in the pride of honest bitterness—and I understood
the words "forlorn" and "desolate," and thus became a wick
up which—for misery loves company—the sorrows
of the greater world deployed their best examples, sorrows
sometimes so more vast than mine—the woman
whose child was born without a brain
inside the saltwater smear of its cranium—that anything,
a sudden drop in temperature of five degrees, a cat that keens
for hours from some mystery distress, could send me
spinning toward the edge of an unmanly weeping, and so
I required an antidote, I knew that as instinctively as dogs
know when to swallow grass and thus encourage vomiting,
and I got in the car, this car, this fast American
panacea, out to where the empty outskirts-driving
gives a sacred feeling of forever to the road, and there, the more I took
on speed, the more the speed took *me,* the more I *was*
a supersonic ripple on the surface of the dopamine
and the serotonin sugaring the night, and by the time I switched
the radio to oldies rock at sound that matched the speed
—that double-whammy formulation of an irresistible,
irrepressible (and, quite frankly, irresponsible) middle-brow transcendence—
I was howling, I was rabbinically werewolf *howling*
to the mileage and its partner-in-crime-and-holiness,

the bass-line beat, and I was born to run, and I was born to be wild,
bad to the bone, and born free (free as the wind blows), I was unashamedly
boomer, I was rocketing the stars and davening gloriously
at the Wailing Wall of the hungry heart, my marrow
was a queen bee's royal jelly of delight, and I was speeding,
I was erasing the planet's grief, I was a wave of plasma physics,
I was the dark gleam on the pungent roe in a slit in a fish
going back to the Paleozoic, I was speeding, and I had no destination,
forward impetus was *itself* the destination, I was unrepentantly
speeding, I was surely exoneratably speeding,
officer.

That's what I wanted to say.

Emma (and Others)

Emma (Mrs. Charles) Darwin

For these thoughts,
his immortal soul would burn like a pinch of tinder,
forever—this man she loved and admired,
and so for forty-three years her house of a heart
continued to keep this fear in its cellar,
chained down there, where the mewling couldn't be heard.

The underworld. Its secret
Persephone sadness. Everyone has sensed
a touch of this grievous song,
sibilant, tectonic,
coming up from the pit to the surface of Earth.
Everyone understands. My friend Joellen:

even ten years later, even watching
the nine-year-old and the seven-year-old
engrossed in their goofy inscrutable play,
the stillbirth isn't buried so deep
in her brain that its ghostly wail doesn't rise
some nights through the cranial graveyard,
muffled by a hand of willful ganglia
across its mouth, but
loud enough. Somewhere below us,

the ancient bones of an ancient torture chamber.
Somewhere below us, the rue of an ancient love.
Today's news is the miners trapped
in the same dark that the dead know.
Can I hear them crying? I think I can.
And for all I know, if I heard
with the thousand ears of a mountain,
the coal cries too.

The Asparagus Tongs

"Looking absentmindedly through his mail one
morning, [the newly married Charles Darwin] turned
up a letter and inquired with astonishment who
Mrs. Charles Darwin was."

— William Irvine

Another charming anecdote about a culture hero.
But an evil twin to a story like this would be
the one of the man whose upper cranium was sheared off
by the rotor into, eventually, a healed-over
neurological parody of a functioning brain, and when
his wife of twenty-seven years—who'd stayed
in the hospital room for two months, day and night,
through all those surgeries—accompanied him
to the therapist's office, and he was asked
to "indicate [his] wife," he stared and pointed
with a trembling and yet seemingly certain finger
"to a small brown vase of twig arrangement,"
disarmingly pleased with this accuracy and unaware
of a woman sitting there sobbing into a Kleenex. It's

the übernightmare version of the common nightmare
Rhoda says she wakes both from and to: "He's there
in the bed, our legs are touching, for eleven years just this way
our legs have been touching, in the moonlight I can see
every pore on his cheek, and yet I realize if he can do
what he did at that party—Albert, don't pretend
you didn't hear—THEN I DON'T KNOW THIS MAN"—which is to say:
an inch away, he floats unknowable astronomical distance off,
in anybody-space, the way the heads of all of us are sealed capsules
of a Schrödinger or Einstein "thought experiment": if a photon
is placed in a shut, unbreachable box that's then sent
hurtling through the universe faster than light, is it a photon
or a hyena or a go-go girl or a suppurating saint? No one
will ever solve that locked room. And did Darwin really know

his children?—ten of them, a lot of vitiation
of a life's attention. Did he know his father, that
portentous, wrathful, overshadowing man? The things
we don't know come in calibers from pebble-in-the-snowball
up to howitzer and more, and there's one certainty we cherish
that's assigned to the blammopower of each. Darwin on the barnacle
is worlds away from Darwin on a wedding present: "Herbert
sent me a massive silver weapon, which I thought
was to catch hold of soles and flounders, but Erasmus tells me
is for asparagus." Those silly men of genius, eh!
He intimately scrutinized the wilds and the strata
of the world—but wasn't worldly. And if Freddie is
a debonair, resourceful, owns-his-own-jet connoisseur
of the human parade, if he assumes command
with ease and charm . . . it didn't work (ask Rhoda) at that party

(I spare you the details), where he knew what's what,
and he knew who's who, but he didn't know shit. Now something is dead
in her, is salted and pinned to a board, with a little label. So
many ways to weep into a Kleenex!—some of them don't even require
weeping and a Kleenex. When the word arrived that his father
had died, Darwin at first was lost in an immensity
as large as geologic time, and couldn't clamber out of it
into dailiness, into the light; but then he retired
for a week to his study, there amid the dots
of algae-swimmers in their dishes, and the South American eel
time had mummified into hawser rope, and the skull of an ape
that fortified the candle-glow in its sockets
into something like a thoughtfulness . . . and he took some consolation
from the fathers of us that he did know.

With Quotes from William Irvine's Account of
the 19th Century Scientist-Explorer Thomas Huxley's Life

I.

"Australian natives believed that white men were
reincarnated ghosts of the dead."

Well we're not.
And yet, in the time and the place invoked,
and given the reigning consensus reality,
given the lack of better or even competing explanations . . .
a very plausible theory.
As good as the physicists' one
about eleven dimensions, about the place where light
is eaten to its pit, about the edge of time,
the end of time, the bubble-cluster cosmos.
Einstein's theory of relativity.
The theory that the hotter the woman,
the bigger an asshole the boyfriend is.
The higher the office, [choose your own:
the huger the graft; the harder the fall].
Gravity waves. The "etherium." ESP.
The theory the burglars *will* be fooled
by our leaving the radio on.
The theory that, no matter the distance,
your spouse is faithful.
(Maybe your spouse's hungers will be fooled
by your leaving your love on.)
In one anecdote about Huxley, his biographer introduces us
to Edward Forbes, "a genial and talented geologist
with a romantic weakness for assuming lost continents
to explain peculiarities of plant and animal distribution."
As if we could posit the sunken Atlantis
exerting its force in the background, and: *bingo:*
marsupials! Why not?—does it *really* sound sillier
than "continental drift"? And Heaven. . . .
Heaven is a theory—not a persuasive one,

I'm afraid, and yet a populous one;
among its throng of billions are my parents,
waving down at me with gusto—theoretically.
But I prefer the actual ones, she with her quiet strength
and her plastic "cigarette" (to wean her away), and he
in his undershorts yukking it up to hold
the thousand fears of our two-bit urban existence at bay . . .
I suppose I even prefer the actual Blackie
to any posited Blackie-in-the-afterlife, although
when I was ten that shrill, pugnacious puff
of a mongrel dog—a snapper and a sneak—made every
day of the year a trial. When he'd run away, and I thought
good!—it was somehow none the less my job to recover him,
to scout down glass-sherd alleys, to investigate
the webby crawlspace darknesses, until
after hours of sweat and hoarse yelling I'd find him hunkered
and sour in some corner, puking grass up—and for this
no theory was needed, it was nothing
but wild-ass cussedness
behind the peculiarities of this stupid, ugly, dead-end
plant and animal distribution.

2.

"Huxley was still in the midst of his strenuous first lecture course. . . .
    He resisted with difficulty an impulse to howl and crow in class."

It seemed to me that, at my niece's wedding,
more people observed how I look like my father
than offered congratulations to the bride and groom.
My father?—with whom I couldn't agree
on anything? If he said snow
I'd say Sahara. Today I look in the bathroom mirror:
time, it turns out, is a kind of agreement.
There he is, inside my bones, and working his way
from the marrow to the surface. My mother,
as usual, beside him. If ghosts are what remain
of a person's essence after the person is gone,
then children *are* ghosts, and the Australian theory
is proved correct, for everybody, white,
black, yellow, red, and all of those midway
toasty colors we're lately so lustily combining toward.
And if we're born only after a stay
on the island of gill, the island of feather,
the island of all-over downy lanugo, then
yes, then grrr, then let the silt
of these lost and sunken awooo, aghaaar,
these lost these aaawp these chrrr, rahoow,
sk'reeel continents sunken continents sssp
rise fsssh uuunh sunken ahyyyaaa
rise once for their credit.

Goth Boy: An Instruction

The sinuous strands of phosphorescent froth
on crow-black ocean made an ever-snaking light show
so hypnotic, Darwin might have (if he'd been without
a sense of mission stirring from its dormancy) sat mesmerized
on his overhang cliff for hours, until the intrusive touch
of sunrise blanked it out. The finches,

too, sometimes apotheosized his studies
into beauty, into an insularizing cone of beauty
so intense—so rhythmic and so avocado-gold
and smutty-gold and dusky-lemon—he'd forget
his heavy notebook, his hypotheses,
and the specimens in his oilcloth. The same

in reading Audubon: his paints and cedar box
of taxidermy tools awaited, but the danger (or,
we could say, the obeisance) was in fascinated dawdling
over those ebony eddies of luster on a breast, a perfect
currant of an eye, a louse in the fold of a throat . . .
distraction has no bottom limit; and this

makes sense, compounded as we are of ever-feathering
and ever-finer neural threads, and
ever-further-subatomic chainstitch . . . still,
we need to fight against this understandable
propensity to drift away, to smother
in the too-much of the world's detail. Tip #10

in the novice writer's how-to guide, "You have to know when
to stop researching your novel," etc. It's a full-blown wonder
to consider the jungles and deep ravines
of ultraviolet a bee sees, or the field of electrical guides
a shark maneuvers by, but we can't live there:
Darwin shook it off and started up again,

of course, and Audubon. Not so, though,
for the Goth boy down the block—sixteen? let's say
he was sixteen—who with his friends adopted
the kohl-and-whiteface stare of death, the black
cloaked dress of death, its language chilling
into freon, and its websites . . . they all

shook it off, except for him, eventually they all
unpinned their focus from that stasis-point
and started up again. Not him. He stayed on,
as a butler for death; and then as a meal
a butler would serve to death; and finally death
(a knife, a late-night fist of pills, whatever)

ingested him. I mean that in the way a preacher
horrifies the children in his flock—to send a positive
instruction. Here's another example: in 1931
the amazing avian collection of Lord Walter Rothschild
was—to the shock of British scientific circles—purchased
by the American Museum of Natural History:

280,000 birds (including "a peerless collection
of birds of paradise") had to be wrapped for shipping, starting
with a layer of newspaper. Everyday British papers
were used at first; when they ran out, Dutch papers
were substituted, at which it was noted "the work of the packers
speeded up considerably." You see?—now they

could shake it off; and so they started up again. In any case,
the very thought of that work is a marvel: 280,000 birds!
560,000 wings! A single hollow wing bone is a prodigy
of nature's, and a feather is a forest under the microscope.
You could, if you wanted, contemplate such majesty
and intricacy your whole life. You could get lost

in the shaft and the lateral barbicels of a bird of paradise feather
until it *is* a Paradise, whispering its enticement: *stay.* And yet even
in Eden, the world called. Evolution waited. The *Elephant Folio* waited.
Madame Curie . . . Rachmaninoff . . . Billie Holliday . . . waited
on the farther side of the gates. And so they shook it off, those naked
and sweetly knowing two; and headed toward the apple.

The Storm

approaches tornado force, and Skyler and I,
two dutiful Kansans, heed the sirens
and head for the basement. This is a storm
where air reminds us it can kill,
can toss a bull from hand to hand
and deal shingling off a roof like playing cards,
a storm, a sky, an outer space
where even—it reminds us of the news from last year—
Pluto is too small. My wife and I . . . what hope
do we have in the bottom of this shaking structure,
tiny one-time flecks of human atoms
that we are? And so it heartens me
to think of Darwin visiting Stonehenge
—two of my monolithic figures, brought together

for one historic (and also prehistoric)
hullo. How . . . *right,* that Darwin's stature and vision
match themselves to this grand lithoskeleton
of the seasons, this mysterious giant's-sextant
for the travel of our planet out toward the stars!
But what he'd come for ("two hours' rail
and a twenty-four mile drive") were the local worms
of this ground; and while the massive stones continued
pointing at the heavens, he was kneeling
on a patch of dirt, to watch the humble geniuses
at work, aerating soil on their journeys
that are also their digestions, and architecting
their pebble-lined burrows: how important they are
both on and in the earth.

Dynamics

The earth unfists a rising warmth of thermals;
then the cold front tumbles in. The Creation tradition;
and the Darwinian. Arguing

all night long. The jingoistic; and the pancultural.
The integrity of cellulose; and the termite.
All night long it rains. One story

to the eroded banks.
A different one to the delta.

The Poem of the Dance of the Real

"The dingo and the Amblyrhyncus wander cheerfully in
the gloomy forests of metaphysics."
                              – William Irvine, on Darwin's correspondence

Dying is life—the last of it,
but life, with its song, its colorectal flora,
its physics. *Death* is metaphysics:
i.e., we can only speculate. Whatever it is (if "is"
is even a state for it) exists ("exists") beyond
empirical knowledge. And this is a poem

against the insubstantiality of speculation.
This is a poem that asks for something real
in the hand, a tuber as sprouted with arms as an Indian god,
a saxophone, a gunnysack, a dingo.
I know, of course, the glory (and, at special times,
the *bingo!* insight and resultant functionality)
of the most empyrean levels of metaphysical conjecture:
Darwin's willingness, let's say, to float

for years inside that broth of air and thought,
thought and air, inside abstraction to the rarefied degree
his mind could purify it to, until
its final condensation had explained our us

to us. And even so, this space
devoid of noun and gravity and volume was preceded
(and sometimes accompanied) by that other space,

in which he'd shake "the great entangled roots"
of a batch of sea kelp, and record its salty population
spanking out, "a pile of small fish,
cuttle-fish, crabs of all orders, sea-eggs, star-fish,
molluscs, and crawling nereidous animals."

He'd dig his hands into the pried-apart chest of a tortoise
and comb the tissues there as comfortably
as someone cleansing a lettuce. And this is a poem

that asks to embrace the stink of his barnacles,
the material over the im-. Even the goofy,
even the hoity-toity, the lowbrow
and the preposterous. Surely the wombat is there.
The spotted dick is there. The trumpeter swan
and the carpenter ant. They're surely dancing
the great dance of the real through the Van Allen Belt
and along the Islets of Langerhans. Come,

my cassowary and smelt, my stars
both dwarf and giant, my Goliath beetle
and buff-chested grouse. If the Amblyrhyncus wanders,
does the Wanderrhyncus amble?
Perhaps. But this is a matter for speculation,
which we must leave to others for now
and go gallivant with the dingo.

"A great volume

might be written, describing the inhabitants of one
of these beds of seaweed."

— Charles Darwin

Inside is a seaweed city of windmills
tilted at, and charged, by a doofus platoon
of seaweed Don Quixotes. A thousand
small green desperations attach
to their deep-green Anna Kareninas and Madame Bovaries,
saline, ululating with the tides. A seaweed
Leopold Bloom is perennially making his seaweed rounds.
A seaweed Gilgamesh is heroic and foolish and torn
at the root by mortality, like anyone.

. .

And my friends are packing the children's lunch,
and into that paper bag goes an irrational premonition
of the bus off the side of the bridge, in flames, and such love
as the carbohydrates and sugars inside of the apple
could never contain if even multiplied by a grove.
"Look here"—a friend is opening up his attaché case
at the sales division's profit assessment meeting; if
we had our special glasses we could see the bats
that boil from this vent, and could appreciate how
the lining of this case is silk in a pattern of roses
splattered from a vein. My friend with the travel pack
of sex toys (should she tuck it into her check-in luggage
or treat it as a carry-on?)—Delilah, Lady Chatterly,
and Eve are in there, the Muses are in there, Cleopatra
and Mata Hari and Salomé and Venus are in there. What
do I make of the two worlds that exist when I find
my father's synagogue bag in a bottom drawer, a bag
of velvet so majestically blue he must have believed it implied
a line of kingship going back to the Temple of Solomon?—in one world

it weighs just the close-to-nothing that you'd guess
a folded prayershawl and a yarmulke would come to;
in another world, the iron of millennia of suffering
is in this bag, in ingots the size of caskets; and a trove
of bars of gold for the lions and cherubim over the altars;
and a wind that begins at the pit of the earth
and carries the song of a people.

• •

spiral wrack, sea potato, sea lettuce, purple laver,
oarweeds, dulse, sea tangle, horsetail kelp,
sea colander, rockweed, long-stalked laminaria,
sea wrack, sugar kelp, channeled wrack, knotted wrack,
bladder wrack, winged kelp, devil's aprons

universes in universes

• •

One of those nights with good wine and companionship
where the high-minded bullshit accumulates.
Sid offered *Uncle Tom's Seaweed,* stopped, then added
Seaweed Dick. (Amanda had read the Darwin quote
aloud, to jumpstart conversation.) Thalia:
The Decline and Fall of the Seaweed Empire. Gravity's Seaweed.
Anything, if you *really* look at it: *anything.*
"Valerie Allen has written *On Farting:*
Laughter and Language in the Middle Ages." (Jokes galore.)
Birds, said Doyle. Birds in mythology, birds in art,
in ornithology, "When a bird flew up my skirt,"
said Olivia, birds in dreams, "In cooking" (Gerta),
in animated cartoons, "Wow," Thalia again, "You could write
a substantial book about birds!" (this blurted
half in an innocent wonder and half as a way of going *duh,*
you ninnies belaboring obvious truths) and Eddie

the self-appointed dry wit of the group said "You could also write a substantial book about up Olivia's skirt."

• •

Rockweed will grow up to seven feet tall, its stalks are the equivalent of tree trunks in a glade. Long-stalked laminaria have stems that can go up to twelve feet long, with fronds of twenty feet, and in their holdfasts one can find—as in the gnarled roots of a jungle forest tree—voluminous life, furtive, exotic, explosive, scampering or siphoning about its own undersea business, fringed or finny or clawed or gluey-footed or foppishly, whippishly tentacled. For example, the rock-borer clam that, "working entirely by repeated and endless mechanical abrasion with its sturdy shell, is said to bore rocks that even resist mechanical drills." The scale worm is protected in armor plating. The fish swim weavingly through these weeds as birds would fly among the boles of a forest, fish as mardi-gras-colored as jungle cockatoos, as exorbitant in display as birds of paradise. Brittle-star and golden-star abound, and scuttling crabs are this world's rodents. Hunting, hiding, appeasing hunger, reproducing: common rhythms are the same here, and as dire and violent (or somnolent) as they are in any ecosystem on land.

The frill of the sugar kelp is edged in a powdery white that gives its name. The horsetail kelp is consisted of lengthy satiny ribbons of a lustrous mahogany brown. In the Pacific there are kelp that rise 150 feet from the bed to the surface: imagine being a helmeted diver exploring that foreign terrain, imagine stepping across a floor-growth of red algae, under the canopies of shadowing fronds, among the "trunks" of these undersea giants. There are tinier wonders as well. The tip of each point of a golden-star creates an infinitesimal current funneling down, drawing in a constant supply of nutrients and oxygen. It's all a matter of scale; given a human perception apportioned to those glassily sinuous, hula-hipped shapes, we might see forms as shocking as the waterspout that once, my friend John says, dipped down like a petulant goddess and lifted a six-man sailboat out of the water, tossing it carelessly over her shoulder; or the pillars of flame and darkness that followed the Israelites

through the desert, towering up from the sands to where their upper
vortices sucked greedily at the heavens.

• •

Every weekday morning: mothers usually, every now and then
a father, bringing a child (or two) to the schoolbus stop,
some skipping with them, laughing; some steadfastly dragging
the little recalcitrant so-and-sos; but all of them, whether
gleeful or half-comatose, aware of the fragile existence
in their care; and of the gates of hell in people's breasts;
and the dice of chance that thunder through the clouds
on even the mildest day; and the dreams we have
that could be carved of alabaster and set on the plains
with beacons of fire inside their eyes that ships would see
from a dozen miles offshore, but that more likely are in
the silences of everyday people lined up for everyday tasks.
And then later the train pulls up, and the mommies and daddies
are office workers off to feed eight hours
of themselves to the various furnaces. The afternoon
my mother said the cancer had metastasized—that colonies
had left her lungs and were working their way across—I put
my ear against her shoulder . . . and I heard the clash of swords,
and the screams of the pierced, and the quiet infrequent
moments of dignity speckled throughout that melee,
and the terror of smoke-blind chariot horses,
and ships in the storm, and families sundered. . . .
She was so small. How could the entire
Iliad have been fit in there?

"Humboldt," says Darwin, "has given a most interesting
discussion on the history of the common potato."
Time to bend down to the dirt and read
the eons inside of those eyes.

Charles's Compliment

Villagers in southern India are worshipping a frog that
constantly changes colour. Zoology professor Oomen V.
Oomen from Kerala University said that he hoped to
collect the unusual frogs for study.

– Fortean Times

Sorry, but I beat you
to that stupid joke, "the oomen condition,"
"oomenkind," blah blah. Such lazy comedy aside,
I think that those could be the terms for what we are
when what we are is in collusion
with the universe at its most absurd and wonder stuffed
. . . its froggiest, we might say,

that erratically chromatic one
from Thiruvanathapurum, Kerala, India
as example. Also the great humdinger rain of frogs
on June 12, 1954, in Sutton Coldfield, Birmingham:
Mrs. Sylvia Mowday says, "My four-year-old daughter
put her little red umbrella up and we heard hundreds of them thudding it—
    coming down

like snowflakes. All our shoulders were covered."
Also the recklessly daredevil frog who hopped straight into a cheetah's jaws
("We *heard* the crunch," said a Colonel McCrumley, and he
was "roundly supported" in this by others) and then a moment later
hopped straight out again, "unscathed." Is this, as one
observer opined, "a miracle?" And Holly: is she

a miracle? Well, I can't parse the implications
of that baggaged word, but I can tell you she rode
her motorcycle straight into the monster jaws
of a twenty-seven-car pileup, was thrown
to the ground, and twice run over: *twice run over,*

her pelvis broken at five points, and a shoulder
and arm and hand and leg were shattered

like flung milk glass: *but her head wasn't touched*
in all this, "not by a hair," "unscathed,"
"a miracle," and if not quite that, still surely
—as she settles into her motorized chair and demonstrates
some kickass zigzag wheelies—she's a nexus
where our lives, no matter how ordinary, also serve
as portals into astonishment. The small frog

Darwin wrote about in Rio de Janeiro moved by suckers
at the tips of its toes and "could crawl up a pane
of glass." It voiced "a pleasing chirp. When several
were together they sung in harmony on different notes"
—not glorious, not a portal, but a tiny chink
in the rock-face wall of the commonplace, through which the amazing
first begins to spill. And once it did for him,

it wouldn't stop: the fossils alone would serve
to make his famous *Beagle* voyage a five-year sentence
punctuated repeatedly by dropping jaw and popping eyes:
one, a skull capacious enough to be scoured out
and used as a baptismal basin; one, no more than a line
of penciled emphasis under a single word in a college text.
"A tolerably perfect head of a megatherium . . . .

A large piece of the tessellated covering like that of an armadillo,
but of gigantic size." These knobs, imprints, and laminae
are indices of another world that enters our world
only through heavy digging—or in dreams. One skull requires
its "animal matter [to be] heated in the flame of a spirit-lamp;
it burns with a slight flame"—and his face is transported
rapturously at this rare occasion. I tell him,

however (in my head we're walking together
around the duck pond in back of his house), the bed sheets
after my wife has left for work are also a fossil
and, for me, no less extraordinary for being
daily and close. He says there *should* be a term for people
when we partake of Cosmic Mystery . . . and I explain
enough of that frog to suggest "the oomen species."
"Very good," he says. "That's very good, Albert."

Everyday People (2)

Zones

There are bootprints on the moon, as permanent
as airlessness provides for; she's seen photographic proof,
their tread an orderly, distinctly human
grid left in the dust . . . and yet she can't influence
Chino's heart just one inch on the other side
of his sternum: and she thumps, as if to prove it,
the chest of her obdurate sixteen-year-old son,
his drugs, his whores, his what-not, while
he stares at her through a mask-of-a-face then
turns away to something more important. Later
I leave too; I drive back home, eleven city blocks
is a million miles away. Who knows and who knows

and who ever knows? A delivery girl at the airport
with a box, *Hand Carry Only* *HUMAN EYES*, and
yawning as if she holds a baggie of burgers. Who
believes, at this late date, that any politician's face
betrays a single clue of emotion any more
than gold face-plates of ancient Cretan sea-kings
in a museum case? The light comes down
as probing as it is in a police interrogation room.
The light comes down as tossed, as unreliable, as it is
in a storm-shook linden tree. Spectroscopy: "we know more now
about the composition of the stars than, say, what constitutes
an act of love in the house across the street."

Struck Together

(with a quotation from Sean Russell's novel *Gatherer of Clouds*)

A day from its discovery,
no one questions seeing Jesus Christ

in a stain, the blood of a river duck
in the fine, blond chopping-block grain.

The week before this, he was immanent in a similar way
in a knot on junk-shop lathing—it's

his tender and corrective stare and his leonine hair,
alright. A surge of Zeus

through the neural circuitry of a common swan . . .
of Adonai in the cellulose of a Sinai desert bush . . .

such thumping drama in religious myth! But the story
of unalike elements struck together

into wholeness is an everyday story as well.
The way the tidy and unwavering command of wrist

in Japanese tea ceremony *is* the formal
death-thrust in the dust of the *corrida*: only

scale differs, only the size of light
around the expertise. The saint who sups

on lepers' pus; the orgiast eating up his lovers'
cheesiest nooks. Today, in the kitchen, a woman

fixes dinner—river duck, in a thick
cilantro cream she's read about—and every hack

of blade against the bone works out another
fresh resentment that she feels toward the man.

Outside, he's sketching at the clouds
of this various summer sky: the cauliflower one,

the one like a bellicose message
breaking into Morse code . . . every cloud becomes her face

he lectures sternly. Still, she calls him in
to see the Christ that squinting makes apparent

in the wood: they share the joke of this
and later, after TV news's zoom-up shot,

they share a week of the curious and the devout
on their front lawn. The angers never disappear

and yet they share, and they share: of course
they share, of course we're the combustion engine

driven by the genes. How could we think or feel
otherwise?—flesh that we are, atoms of flesh that we are,

infinitesimal machinery-parts of negative charge
and positive charge in a system

that we are. And this is its diagram:
Coming to a tree trunk that curved out almost horizontally

over the water, Shonto stopped and leaned against it.
Nishima circled its base and leaned against

the opposite side. . . . They stayed like that,
side by side facing opposite directions.

Honeycomb, Calling

Everything inside it was the tiny, regimented motion
of jewels in the case of an eighteenth-century Swiss watch;

then it called out to its opposite—a seemingly unavoidable
law of nature—and the brute swipe of a huge bear

in a hungry shamble cracked that hive
in two: its honey glistening the way

we imagine the lining of the heart would
when exposed to light. And now

that the poem has somehow found its place
inside a forest, *it* calls too . . . and in response

we have its other self, the edgy urban lyric,
where the factories sag, and the gang crest of the week

is two crossed needles over a field of poppies,
and everyone's favorite, Smog Boy and the Terrorist Belles,

is playing at the wiggle-up-close-and-personal club.
—Which is, by the way, where the man and the woman

inside this poem first met, and made,
like plus and minus, heat and cool,

the parts of a binary system. Maybe the trouble,
he thinks, as he sits at the pier in an after-battle funk,

is that they called it love. The night is chill
and woos the comfort straight out of his shivering body.

The night is chill and long. The moon is arid, and wants,
and lifts, the oceans of this planet.

Whatever Surrogate

Because we were evolved to rush for berries in the dark,
avoiding predators eight times our weight and speed, and *now*
we have that same emotionalenergyturmoiloompahpah
of endless need and heat and promise in our selves, but not enough
of daily circumstance in which to invest it, in which to burn it
away . . . well, we have church, and boxing, and Oscars,
and philandering . . . whatever surrogate extraness suffices.
In the ring tonight, the two contenders circle
unceremoniously, and then begin the pugilistic
razoring that's what a cockfight *is.* The three-inch
emerald-and-silver attachments savage flesh, and
the Japanese tea ceremony, the bibliophile's eBay wars,
the corrida, the tenure committee, the rooster gore
that sparkles in the dirt like fallen piñata candy.

Photographs of the Interiors of Dictators' Houses

It's as if every demon from hell with aspirations
toward interior design flew overhead and indiscriminately
spouted gouts of molten gold, that cooled down
into swan-shape spigots, doorknobs, pen-and-inkwell sets.
A chandelier the size of a planetarium dome
is gold, and the commodes. The handrails
heading to the wine cellar and the shelving for the DVDs
and the base for the five stuffed tigers posed in a fighting phalanx:
gold, as is the samovar and the overripe harp
and the framework for the crocodile-hide ottoman and settee.
The full-size cinema theater accommodating an audience
of hundreds for the screening of home (or possibly
high-end fuck flick) videos: starred in gold
from vaulted ceiling to clawfoot legs on the seating.
Of course the scepter is gold, but the horns
on the mounted stag heads: do they need to be gilded?
Yes. And the olive fork and the French maid's row of dainty buttons
and the smokestack on the miniature train
that delivers golden trays of dessert from the kitchen
to a dining hall about the size of a zip code,
and the snooker table's sheathing, and the hat rack,
and those hooziewhatsit things in which you slip your feet
on the water skis, and the secret lever
that opens the door to the secret emergency bunker.
Smug and snarky as we are, in our sophisticated
and subtler, non-tyrranical tastes, it's still
unsettling to realize these photographs are also full
of the childrens' pictures set on a desk,
the wife's diploma proudly on a wall, the common
plastic container of aspirin, and the bassinette
with the scroll of linen shade at the ready
in case the sun is too powerful: reminders of how
a graduated continuum connects these überoperatically
fat interior lives to our own. We all desire
"more" and "better," Melville adds that final "e"

to the family name, and Faulkner adds the "u," in quest
of a signified gentility. My friend Damien
(fake name) won A Certain Literary Award, and
at the stellar after-ceremony party, in the swank hotel's
swank atrium, he found a leggy literary groupie
noshing caviar under a swankily lush mimosa,
and in under an hour his own swank room could boast
the golden statuette, the evening's loveliest woman, *and*
the silver serving platter of five-star caviar,
and *if* you think this story's moral lesson is
that satiation is ever attained, you don't understand
the protoknowledge we're born with, coded into our cells:
soon soon soon enough we die. Even before we've seen
the breast, we're crying to the world that we want;
and the world doles out its milkiness in doses. We
want, we want, we want, and if we *don't* then
that's what we want; abstemiousness is only
hunger translated into another language. Yes
there's pain and heartsore rue and suffering, but
there's no such thing as "anti-pleasure": it's pleasure
that the anchorite takes in his bleak cave
and Thoreau in his bean rows and cabin. For Thoreau,
the Zen is: wanting less *is* wanting more.
Of less. At 3 a.m. Marlene (fake name) and Damien
drunkenly sauntered into and out of the atrium,
then back to his room: he wanted the mimosa too,
and there it stood until checkout at noon, a treenapped testimony
to the notion that we will if we can, as evidenced in even
my normally modest, self-effacing friend. If we can,
the archeological record tells us, we'll continue wanting
opulently even in the afterlife: the grave goods
of pharaohs are just as gold as the headrests
and quivers and necklace pendants they used every day
on this side of the divide, the food containers
of Chinese emperors are ready for heavenly meals

that the carved obsidian dragons on the great jade lids
will faithfully guard forever. My own
innate definition of "gratification" is right there
in its modifier "immediate," and once or twice
I've hurt somebody in filling my maw. I've walked
—the normally modest, self-effacing me—below a sky
of stars I lusted after as surely as any despot
contemplating his treasury. The slice of American cheese
on the drive-thru-window burger is also gold,
bathetically gold,
and I go where my hunger dictates.

A Few of the Ways to Say It

Of course there's pain. How could it be
otherwise? The first rule of the universe is
that it's meant to contain all things.

. .

And the scar . . . ?
The universe works through its constituent parts.
When pain is required—the same
as when joy is required, or quiet devotion—
then some of us are called upon.
The scar is a sign of the system working.

. .

Hers . . . I never knew its story.
I only knew it was there—this thin dead inch—
in a crease where I thought of her
as being most open to intensity.
A death part . . . isn't that what the scar is?
The first of us—the lemming of us—
to leap off into that realm.

. .

I'd lick it. Well, to be accurate . . .
I'd lick everything
including it. The tongue,
going slowly enough, is always a knowing
paleontologist.
It would halt, and linger, and try to read
the life back into that fossil.

. .

And the tongue could arouse her
in one place; then another place; another place. . . .

But not here.
Here, the gospel stopped.
There was no resurrection here.

       • •

A final way to say it.
One night, a night that included a party
of fashionistas and video coverage, she
uncharacteristically devoted an hour to her makeup.
When she was done she wasn't susceptible
to anything, not in this new self.
And so I understood what "scar" is then . . . that pale
impervious surface: this is the geisha face
of the wound.

Our Argument, Like the Thunderstorm,

is over. Like the thunderstorm,
a drizzle continues to drip from the leaves.

Is the sun a god? It used to be a god.
And that would make these clouds
its acolytes—how even once it's set
below the hill line, effectively buried,
they continue to reflect
the gospel of sun throughout the neighborhood.

So: remnants.
The confetti left after the bachelorette party.
The leftover wood from the whittler's competition
that was used to jam open the jaws
of a buried vampire in the village's cemetery.
The sweet but muskily pungent molecules of onion
still on the fingertips of the cook.
There was a Big Bang, out of Nothing, and
some recombined units of energy out of that maelstrom
are reading this now.

And you may call these bed sheets
if you want—but the experts in sex and in anger
can recognize them for a fossil.

Out of the sheep, its gut.
Out of the gut, these strings.
And in the hands of the dutiful child practicing
at his music—and not completely
devoid of pleasure—a kind of bleating resumes.

That Re- (What We Are)

Seventh grade, the boy is set to memorizing one
of Shakespeare's sonnets, and he reads it and rereads it
—it becomes his cud—with slow deliberation
. . . not unlike the way the planet itself millennially repeats
its several stories, the Flood (or the Fire);
the Virgin Birth (or raised by animals); the various quests;
the reason for death; the reason for kneeling to deity;
the war against the Other (even dwindled to the pissy
little skirmishes of spouse opposing spouse): right now
he's dawdled home from school and interrupts them
at the fang-and-claw crescendo of a battle
(his strip-clubbing with the guys . . . her shopping frenzies . . .) they resort to
with the hunger of a junkie for the rush . . . the way,
perhaps, Van Gogh became a living smoulder of addiction

for the sexual arousal of the wheat, by the wind; for the crows;
for the infurled nebulae with which creation
fingerprints the sky. He couldn't *not* redo such majesty
each day—nor could his brain (nor mine, nor yours) refuse
to dream the day each night, in shuffled repetition.
"Let me not to the marriage of true minds
admit impediment" indeed; the easy irony
between his chosen sonnet and this household's sets of tension
isn't lost on the boy, and neither is the old, enduring
comfort: we can find him—big shot, lover man,
oh cool, cool, up-yours, kickass man—in bed by 8 p.m.
in the fetal position. And who knows?—Van Gogh might have studied
a local girl asleep in his bed in exactly that curl, before
ascribing its beautiful infurl to his nighttime sky. This

shape . . . this inescapable and iterative gesture . . .
it's ubiquitous in us . . . the *re-* of *-flex* and *-ply* and *-capture*.
If we see it in the reenactor's surface authenticity (although
she's flossed her teeth and shaved her armpits) as a Renaissance

high lady in attendance at a (rubber-blunted) joust . . .
and in a reincarnate ancient Grecian priestess
whose oracular announcements ululate from her and vie
with the nineteenth century's skreel of London traffic . . .
-view, -spond, -vise, -connoiter . . . well, of course:
what *are* we anyway, if not the means
—the chromosomal means—by which Creation takes its elements
in hand again, and does another encore? So: ontogeny.
So: every grudge and glory day a woman in a bar rehearses
for anyone who will listen. We're the small, backpedal touch

that keeps the universe from flying into entropy too quickly.
*What's the rush? The speed of light will wait. My mind is a bounty
of reruns.* For the universe, that's sound survival strategy.
For us it's not so simple, and the pleasures we revisit
are a measure of the equal count of hellishness we've suffered through,
that haunts us back. Who *hasn't* been this boy on the bed at 8 p.m.
in a U-turn curve of his body, imploring
some vague power to readmit him into the insular safety
of the womb? This boy; this *re-ostat* for gauging
a desire to travel against the current of time, and start
anew. On his bed. With his series of sobs
that shame him. Under his poster of a Van Gogh afternoon
so painfully bright, the sun is a cauldron overspilling sheets
of molten gold . . . the same sun under which there's nothing,

Shakespeare tells us, new. Now having reincorporated those earliest
subsets of the poem back into its fold (the boy, the Bard, the artist
unswervably true to his cosmos) you might think we were done;
and yet that mumbling woman in the bar—that recollector
of the shards of her own life—insists we linger a minute.
Someone loved her once. Somebody licked along the blue vein in her throat
and found it lovely. Someone spent an hour counting every pulse
of travel up a blue-gray artery of hers, and found it

lovely, and thought of the lovely rhythm of salmon leaping
up the blue of their stream—chinook and sockeye and silver—
once, in northern Oregon, and the light that flashed, in moments,
on their mail was a wonderful thing, but it was brutal as well
to see them bruised up the ladders, some of them rags,
compelled as they were to return to the source.

The Nose in Feet

"Estimated length of human nose removed by U.S.
plastic surgeons each year, in feet: 5,649."

– Harper's Index

My friend W's daughter got rid of 169 pounds
last year. Now you're supposed to say, "Wow,
how did she do it?" and then I answer (ta-daa!)
"She got divorced." A very sad ta-daa,

by the way, but not an unusual one: the American pounds
lost on this diet every year add up to . . . I don't know,
but the annual total of knifed-off nose
"exceeds the length of George Washington's nose on Mount Rushmore"
by a factor of 260, and so I imagine the grief
that climbs the scales in divorce courts
easily weighs as much as the graft of any five consecutive presidencies, or
(in misery units) a full Fort Knox of piled misgivings.
And what the plastic surgeons do with the daily residue
of their practice . . . save it for stem cell research?
sell it as goo to the hungry makeup industry?
or simply sweep it into an incineration dumpster? . . . I don't know,
I don't even know what I did with the breaths

of *no* and *no* in response to the rabbi's urgent
please and *please,* but there was Simply No Way
that my thirteen-year-old brain on fire with poetry
and girls and an upstart humanism was going to commit
to the dowdier world of *yeshiva* study, and now
I think it's not impossible those breaths became
a small stone in the Wailing Wall, where the old Jews
knock their foreheads on that cool slate-gray solidity
as proof of something ethereal. And the Taj Mahal? . . .
is arguably the world's most grandiose love poem: so
is that where my broken promises to Sylvia went,
and my pleasure in lazily studying Gloria's rump

as the butter of afternoon sunlight poured across it . . .
are these a couple of sky-blue beads of water in a reflecting pool,
a couple of atoms of gilding on a cornice? And the tapes
that Nixon conveniently "lost," the documents the Bush administration
shredded and shredded and shredded . . . go back
into history and consider the contents
of all of those boxes heave-ho'd over the side of what
becomes the official record . . . enough, don't you think, for us
to construct an alter-White House, one of secret shame,
surrounded by alter-equestrian statues of national heroes
rearing up, mid-deed. It's all the lesson
we were supposed to have mastered in eighth-grade science:
the things we think we lose

are merely repositioned. Into a different lover, maybe.
A cold front, muscling in from the tundra. A coin.
The rockface bearing the prominent visages
of prominent Americans, maybe. The Universe
on its upper case level keeps stable, no matter
the shufflings in our dear brief lower case lives.

If W's daughter really did shed 169 pounds
of herself . . . she wouldn't exist
(she's only a lithesome 120 pounds) and minus-49 pounds
would be hovering overhead, and keening to mark this eerie loss,
a miniature astronaut of antimatter.
Maybe that's the problem . . . I mean, at 120 pounds

a young and willowy woman has many options, maybe
too many, maybe too ooh-la-la-and-wink-wink beckoning possibilities
in the stripmalls and the alt-rock concert halls
and the biker barrooms and the open-mic nights of America,
and at every location another pound of him
was left in a corner, an ounce of memory here,

a peck of fealty there. . . . He may have done
the same, kept her on a kind of mental travois
dragged behind: at every bump on his trail
a pound was jostled off, until 120 bumps
completely undid her. So is that what happened?
I don't know. What I do know is how dark it is

tonight in W's living room, with only a blinds-slit thinness
of the moon to show how weary he is
of this going-nowhere talk; and to show his wife's
enormous sadness written across her face in veins
like old-time schoolbook lessons in penmanship,
Love fails, Love fails, Love fails; and their daughter . . .
has a sort of horribly artificial composure
I think is worse than her grief, that exists to her grief
as a faux fur coat exists to the actual animal . . .
and we sit here—going nowhere—and
our goodwill is so flimsy, though the darkness
is a weight that I can only call monumental.

Altered

"The first in a series of books to follow was *The Tenggren Mother Goose* issued in 1940. From this book forward there was a huge change in Tenggren's style. The makeover was so obvious that there was good reason to speak about a pre- and post-Disney Tenggren style. . . . The books of the fifties and sixties revealed once again a drastic evolution in style."

– Lars Emanuelson, on Gustav Tenggren, the Swedish-American artist
perhaps best known for his vastly popular Little Golden Books
(*The Poky Little Puppy*, etc.) and, earlier, his work
on Disney's *Pinocchio*

And I want a titanium widget drizzled
into a waiting, open mold inside my cerebellum.
And the toot king, Mr. Pussy Hound, is finally reinvented
as a top-bucks marquee Pentecostal exhorter-of-the-flocks,
his sins tucked into his body and reconformed
vestigially, like legs inside the whale.
And I want to see the-node-where-my-integrity-is-stored
performing calisthenics out in the courtyard at dawn,
becoming the ethics version of six-pack-in-a-speedo.
And the minister, Reginald Steele, who his congregation all
call "Stainless" Steele, is caught by snoopy highway troopers
romping wheezily in the back of a stolen van with
someone (judging by her ass tattoo) called Cherri Delyte.
I want, and I want, and I want, ". . . in porn;

but after our commercial break: her second career,
in political office!" We live in fast-track make-over times, we live
in the flux of a metamorphic universe: the free subparticle
reinvented as part of an integral molecule of matter; or the sticky inch
of writhing reinvented, after time in pupal limbo, as a wingéd thing
of airborne grace: who *wouldn't* want such change illumined
heraldically on his family crest! The porn star's name
was Phoenix; now we know why. *I want, I want,* and in the Renaissance

"the ancient [Roman] temples, the Coliseum, the great
memorial arches had been in plain sight for centuries, but now
they were no longer pitiable remnants of paganism; they
were majestic creations to be studied and copied"
(Jacques Barzun): a shiny new identity, as transformed
as those plastic-cats-to-plastic-robot-warriors

my neighbor's child plays with. *I want* . . . I want what
Gustav Tenggren presumably wanted the night he walked to the end
of the cape of Dogfish Head on Southport Island, having left
his mark on all of the Tyrolean design of Disney's *Pinocchio,*
then broken with the studio, and now . . . ah, "now,"
and "next" . . . such simple words, to haunt a man! A seagull
shoulders into the fog, giving up its substance
like a watercolor bird in too much water . . . there's a farther side,
of course, it reemerges from the fog . . . but that's as lost
to Tenggren's vision as the future of his own career. In any case,
he *does* succeed refashioning the "look"—and so
revivifying the soul, the juice, the forward-march
momentum—of his art . . . in kindred spirit to the remarkable
    octogenarian poets
(Hall, Ashbery, Bly and Rich) who are under consideration

in a review by Roger Gilbert: "What all four poets share is
an extraordinary resilience, a trait that has enabled each of them
to go on trying new things, rather than repeating
a single successful formula." But then there's Lois, my friend
whose son and brother died last year. Her life is invested
in stasis, an attempt to see the planet stopped
in the year that *they* stopped, in tribute. So her son's room,
and her brother's toy train workshop: not a pen cap,
not a wisp of wooden shaving, has been moved, nor is our conversation
allowed to stray from their truncated lives: as if we're here
to be a museum of them. And so she's here,
in her extreme way, to remind us: the unchanging

is a universal force as real as change; the two together
are a unified theory of human lives, in which we play

our small representative parts. And me . . . *I want* . . . I want
whatever one wants for the following day, when one has written
the thousandth hopeful poem that serves
the One True Everlasting and Unattainable Poem, then walks to the end
of whatever Dogfish Head exists inside his head, in the fog there,
by the frightening, beckoning, seemingly endless water.
There's a story, a kind of dream, a kind of pancultural dream,
about entering that water, and it manifests itself
in ways specific to many times and many peoples.
In one, the protagonist is searching—or
is proving himself through searching—and he makes a fateful sojourn
through the belly of a water-beast; and is ejected;
and drowns. And when he wakes, his wooden body
is altered to that of a real boy.

Over Miles of Iowa Fields: *Snorkel, Karaoke, Leaf*

She wants her husband dead: *that's* understandable,
he's such a dick. (Small parties of the size that require
the rearranging of restaurant tables sometimes start
their evening by a round of fanciful avenues
toward his demise, each followed with a rousing toast thereunto.)
What we'll *never* understand is why a whole plane is required
to explode, for this accomplishment.
"Collateral damage": i.e., lives, of which the least of them
is as important to itself as is, for instance, Einstein's life,
or Einstein's any afternoon, his head
inside a four-dimension rosette-whirl
of busy chalk equations, like the paw of a bear
exploring in the center of a crowded hive, for honey—for the honey
that's the substrate of the universe; or . . . Cleopatra's morning,
as she lazes to her neckline in a youthifying bath
of scented asses'-milk (such luxury, it looks
as rich as melted tusks) and daydreams
of immersion, too, in the gift that her overachieving
goumba Roman lust-thrall, Antony, delivered
last night from the hold of barges spread along the Nile
like giants' shelves: 200,000 books. . . .
These are the standard examples.
Homer, Rembrandt, Coltrane, Lady Murasaki, Darwin, Rosa Parks.
But I ask you to look at this everday-people-version of hell:

the luggage of the dead, obscenely burst
to reveal their intimacies over miles of Iowa fields.
Here: somebody's travel bag contained a vial—an ounce—
of saffron, which consists of 1,400 tiny stigmas
from the purple crocus, pinched by hand and carefully dried.
Somebody else: the handle that would fit a guide dog's harness
(if we had a machine for measuring trust as it registers
in human sweat . . . how many units have coated this device?).
Somebody else: a published update on the 30-million-year-old bones
of a hummingbird German specialists found,

that wee print of a blur at last invited to share
our time with us. Somebody else: a pair
of lace bikini panties—"seafoam" color according to the label,
and it's true: they look about to evaporate
into the afternoon sun. And each of these: a chapter
in a story of unimaginable profundity. The high gods
in the stars and in the ancient texts soliloquize
their dramas—sacrifice, revenge, creation,
and the rest—in ways that use us
for expression. We're the snorkels
that they breathe through when they play in that difficult medium,
mortality. Listen:
That sonofabitch, if he comes around HERE *once more*—
is karaoke: is our singing of the lyrics
written originally for thunderjolt and fireshower.
Every story, yours, your neighbor's, mine,

bespeaks such urgency and dearness.
Shirley Huang's: against the wall of water
two hundred feet tall, her kayak
appeared like the kind of minor imperfection
easily smoothed from a block of coliseum marble;
and then it crashed on top of her,
"I don't know how, somehow *I* got on top of *it*
and over"—she survived, two broken eardrums
and a cracked rib, she was saved
by a guardian angel's hydromanagerial efforts,
she was saved by an unremembered flash
of the skills in her own subconscious,
of the teethclamp, cuntclench instinct for life
in her own subconscious, and this is a tale she'll tell
and tell until the very repetition deepens it
into legend, she will lifelong be a curator
and a fabulist, a rubricator and bard, of this

most axial and nuclear and aggregate
and everfresh and all in all
astonishing story. And equally self-compelling
of course is the narrative of Competitive Eating champion
Sonya Thomas: 9.76 pounds of lobster
"in only twelve minutes," 32 hot dogs "in only twelve minutes,"
and, "in only nine minutes," 11 pounds of cheesecake.
Someone, somewhere, is a genius in the arena of microdynamics,
is part of "a team of successful scientists
who reported that they have teleported
individual atoms for a fraction of a millimeter." Someone
else, a hero in the annals of enormity:
as recorded in *Byzantine History,* "a copy
of Homer's *Iliad* and *Odyssey* was written in gold letters
on a serpent's intestine 120 feet long." I once met

Marvin Minsky, the man who invented the term
"artificial intelligence." Another person: "feedback loop."
"Prenup." "Swapping spit" for a certain rooty-tooty
juicy kiss. "With the help of a breeze, her hair
confided her neck to the room"—somebody sculpted that
line out of language. Someone is the editor
of *The Journal of Arid Environments,* and someone
is the Professor of Fowl Pathology at an Albanian university.
Karl Peter Paulsen, 56, of Germany, now owns 60,000
ballpoint pens. Josip Galic, 69, of Bosnia,
has four kidneys ("normal in size and fully functional").
For Brenda Archer, 46, of Auckland, New Zealand, the story
is the meteorite, about the size of a grapefruit,
"hot to touch," that broke through the roof
one morning as she was stirring up breakfast—this is a story
with bells and zings and knots of media jerkheads
scraping around on her lawn, but somebody else's story
is simply returning home

from that day's medical procedure, in a mask
of quiet dignity. A simple story could even be
this father and his daughter out to hike
an Appalachian trail, early one day
in a glorious swirl of russet and amber fall.
She's seven: *everything* is interesting! They
like each other, and talk to each other, and really
don't even notice how the shadow of an airplane
is as momentary and delicate on her cheek
as that of a falling leaf.

Round, Polished Stones

> Fadhel al-Maliki, an Iraqi resident in New Jersey, was arrested
> at Los Angeles International Airport . . . a piece of chewing gum
> wrapped with wires was found concealed up his bottom, along
> with "some kind of round, polished stone" that al-Maliki said
> was "from another planet."
>
> — *Fortean Times*

I suspect you're going to say now "Right,
another planet: Uranus." (*I* did.) Still, the gotcha
adolescent humor isn't worth the loss
in accuracy: the "other planet" obviously is Mr. al-Maliki's
not-communally-here-with-the-rest-of-us-Earthlings
head. Although, in full disclosure: which of us, inside us
—in some chancel of the psyche, in some oubliette
dug into the cellular bedrock—*doesn't* hold a secret
inner space as sacred, demonic, or simply incomprehensibly
mysterious as outer space? A Mars is simmering
undetectably bloody-red inside the ignominious schlep
a tatterdemalion beggar is, who's also the returned
Ulysses slinking incognito as he schemes revenge
against the queue of suitors; and a musky, potent Venus
is shrouded away, but surely is rounding into its fullness, mound
by mound, inside the plain and planar lines
of famous girl sleuth Nancy Drew. So if our fictions tell us who
we are, I'm thinking that our minds and mitochondria contain entire
versions of astronomy within, that wait
discovery. As far as "polished stone" goes, Richard Shaver

is its reigning Galileo. In the early 1950s Shaver realized
that the everyday rocks beneath our feet are "books,"
are a library filled with pictures, left here by the Elder Gods
who colonized Earth from the far stars, long before humankind.
He called this "new science" ROKFOGO, and
he dutifully spent twenty years at slicing stone
with a diamond saw, to thinness that allowed him to shine

a light through, thus revealing the lingeried vamps
and lizard monsters and warrior mothers and weird homunculi
and midwife dolphins and men-with-gills and ape-bats
of this hidden pre-prehistory. *As far as I know,*
I am the only one who has ever really looked at any rock
respectfully. So okay, we can say he scores a hundred
on the al-Maliki scale; but that's not to say he isn't, himself,
persuasive of the general truth of his insight: there's more "us" here
than there seems to be us. Compared to Shaver, everyone else
is an amateur backyard astronomer of this realization.
Once, about three decades back, after hours of heated argument
with a girlfriend—so intense it left us limp against
each other as if in afterlove—I rested my head

upon the lion-yellow polished stone she wore
as a pendant between her breasts, and it conducted
into my understanding all of the unvocalizable story
of being her for a day: the static-riddled 24/7
tunnel of dyslexia she traveled through; the mother
with the collection of 500 bracelets, to cover and cover and cover
the razor scars on her wrists; and Dog, the boyfriend
who preceded me, whose trust fund was converted totally
into a whirringly sleepless complex, out in the hills,
of antennae and electrobeamers, awaiting the chance
to signal othergalactic conversationalists. . . . Last night
a TV show with a typically long-limbed Nordic supermodel,
every inch of pale, gemmed, and pampered five-nine stature unnecessarily
boosted in six-inch heels / *click* / and a Bantu pygmy
over her pounding-stone and her millet. . . .
If your *life* depended on coming up with a tally,
if you could straighten its numbers into a flexible line
around the moon and back a dozen times,
a hundred . . . still you couldn't count the planets
that cohabit on this planet.

What We Were Like (2)

The Lamps

What the TV says, and the Web Page says, and the fifteen-member
     Committee
on Reimaging the Product. . . . But I'm thinking

of the story in which the Rabbi is done with the long day's draining
nineteenth-century labor and drops insensible to his sleeping-straw

still wearing the dung-flecked clothes of the field, then suddenly
looks down at himself from the air, the way the bright release

of oil-light must look down at the smudged and heavy glass
for a minute: and then, the Rabbi ascends for the night

through the level of Cloud, and past the sword-bearing Guardians
with their riddles, and finally unto the gates of Eternity itself,

wherein he wanders until his earthly body reels him back
along a thread of *kasha*-steam, which we'd call being

downloaded into hard copy, for this is our language
here, the language of buying and selling the lamps,

and not of releasing the genie.

Perception Poem

The limits of our range. The light our eye can see
is centrist, and another Earth of other light exists
to left and right. The stars that welt across
the sky appear from Mystery and disappear
in the sea in a balancing Mystery—the way
the unexplainable, seared signs of the stigmata do
on a body. No one knows if we (the "we"
of time so distant that we measure its successful reclamation
by a few found femurs) mated with Neanderthals, and
frankly no one's sure if the Dickersons right across
the street mate when the sun goes down
and the shades in their windows correspondingly lower.
And I've heard they used to not have shades, but often
birds would die from the (to them) invisible glass.

• •

"A woman came into the bar," said Marla, "thirty
maybe, very good-looking. So everyone looked.
This really happened: she walked straight up
to the bar itself, and climbed on top at a spot
that was empty of glasses. She just stared ahead,
she didn't make contact with anyone. There
was quiet, as if by consensus. Nobody knew
who she was. She lifted her skirt—there wasn't much
to lift—and bared her pussy; and from out of it she fingered
a diamond, and placed it plunk on the bar top,
and she walked back out." A pause. And then a million
questions fly from our mouths and jostle in the air.
"It was a ten-carat diamond.
And none of us ever learned more than that."

• •

One by one, and errorless, the sightless cave fish
—waxy-white albino slivers—sleek up into the pock
in a rock that's barely bigger than they are,
and through it. Somewhere in there's a metaphor
for us, and what we're blind to, what enormity
we're blind to, and how surely and emphatically we still
conduct our daily selves. The difference is: *they* don't know
that they don't know. Ours is an awful awareness,
filled with itch and wonder. There's a pattern out there
we can't see—not even if we're the threads of it;
or especially. Swift and close enough, those fish become
a single silver thread. A continuity. Our generations
might be lines like that, to the eyes of the universe.
That might be its perception.

Crazy Way

Sometimes hurried, garbled
reading is truest.
"I will work forty hours a week clerking at the painstore."
—from a poem by Donald Hall. I'd rushed,
and glazed over the *t*

and yet my accidental revision
feels right for the crabbed, defensive life
that Hall gives voice to, and in fact
for Ace Digornio, who I knew

when I was a child and who *did*
spend forty hours every week behind the counter
at Talman's Home Decor and Paint Store.
It's the crazy way that misperception has
of walking slantwise toward veracity.
"In medieval bestiaries, for example, scholars [claimed]
that bees are born from an ox's body"—I don't know

about the ox, but I know Ace Digornio
one unforgettable afternoon ran out of the store
and into the lunch-rush traffic, shrieking,
slapping at his chest and saying insects were flying
and burrowing and hatching—*that's*
what got me, insects *hatching*—in his body.
No one ever saw him in public again. And if
those bees in that ox are surely a metaphor
for Ace Digornio, surely he's a metaphor
for all of us—our deep and maybe otherwise
inarticulable suffering. Maybe an eyeleted shoe,
a cello, a used syringe, a lush bouquet of backyard iris . . .
any object is good enough for misery,

and any misreading.
Across the street was a music store.
If you press *piano*'s *o* enough,
the secret pain inside it will rise.

Smallish

A single wing of a *real* angel . . . ? That
would be the travel of light through the universe.
Now imagine *both* wings . . . no, we can't.
Instead, medieval artists set them
onto a figure's shoulders, made a backpack, made them
glorified epaulettes, so that the Annunciation
can fit into Mary's room. One task
of a window is to domesticate the sky.
I make this process sound unappealing, I know,
but that isn't my intention: we're
the atoms of stars, the atoms of what preceded the stars,
reorganized to the confines of Earth: and so
our understanding *needs* to breed for smallness.
It's like "love" or "terror" . . . we require
the smallish people in books and paintings.
Ahab. Anna Karenina. Whitney Houston's songs.
Because we need to outlast hurt,
Audubon has given us this flamingo
patiently waiting on one exactly rendered leg.
Because we must absorb a cosmos
we can't comprehend, we've been given this infant
by Mary Cassatt, who homes in toward the nipple
with complete faith in supply-and-demand.
Le Funk, an uptown dance bar: all the whoopass
and canoodle of the human race seems squeezed inside
this thumping strobe-lit oblong; "I will always love you,"
Whitney Houston sings, although that "always" gets
relayed in under six minutes of deejay time.
The earliest moon we depicted:
was scored on a stone from a creek.
Big stone: little stone.

Off from Shore

Out of all of the foxes in England tonight,
this one, only this one, is loping
across a snowdust-whitened field
on three legs: every minute, the space between it
and the gnawed paw in the trap
increases, not only in linear distance but
in units of dark, dark mystery
and vanquished pain: this fox, this creature come
through its unique determination
and its sacrifice to a place of ascendancy
over the common creatures of this landscape
and their common place on the wheel of hunting and dying.
Elsewhere—not far, in a village where the milk is
still delivered to the stoops in bottles—the cream
has risen in one, a golden crown
awaiting being found in the early light.
And very far away, a butterfly the size of an opened atlas
and the colors of a Persian rug
is floating on the heat plumes of the afternoon:
I have nothing but a city-boy's respect
for the everyday cockroach: its pugnaciousness,
its thug survival skills, and yet I have to acknowledge
this pasha of the insect world
as it effortlessly graces the air.
Everywhere, it seems, we can discern
when the royal arrive among the hoi polloi; in Erie,
Pennsylvania, once, at two or three in the morning,
in a diner where the out-of-luck and out-of-work
and out-of-their-minds collected for the eking-out of coffee
across the perilous hours, I watched as a man
the world would call a drunk bum mumbled his willingness
to assist a woman the world would call
a drunk whore with the sugar packet her own hands
trembled too helplessly with . . . and when she assented,

105

he went about this small task with the gravest concentration
and most flourishful aplomb . . . as if
he'd been given the honor of sweetening a cup of joe
the Pope had ordered, and all of the media screens
of the world were turned to his leisurely, dainty
pour and stir, this son of the son of a son
of pourers and stirrers . . . first apprenticed, then medallioned,
and justly proud of the lineage. Even
among the bunco artists an aristocracy exists.
The pickpockets will not deign to carry a knife:
so crude. The con-scheme fabricators won't pick a pocket:
"It's dirty," one said, as if my pocket might taint his fingers
with smears of industrial sewage. Although I understood
my pocket wasn't dirty, but the stooping
to such base resort. The best, the princes among them,
merely talk. They talk, and the money flows.
They talk and the ruse, the magic story, calls forth jewels
the way the piper's music called the rats
from the flooring in Hamelin town. They talk
the way Scheherazade confabulated away a thousand nights;
they enter a room and even the king is held in thrall,—
the talker may be frail and blind, but he enters a room
and begins, and the shadows give way to the beckoning
wine-dark sea and Odysseus casts off from shore.

The Poppy Fields of Afghanistan

appear overnight in the white gauze
soaking up her wound.
The following morning they wheel in a photograph:
an aerial view of a recent tributary
of the Amazon River, claiming its knotted way
across the ground—it is, they say,
the problem, this is what they need to divert.
All night I've been awake at her side
with the dust of the fallen Babylon
a lament in my throat, and a vision
of meadows of Alpine flowers—as neat
and smooth as lavender velour—for a contrast.
Even here. Yes even
in this room so far removed from the world.

A Typo for "Paths of Gravel" on page 17 of Jack Williamson's
Demon Moon (Tor Books)

As you probably know, there were times
and places in which men took a sacred vow
by placing a hand on their testicles;
hence "testimony." Hence the easy wit
upon seeing a young guy with his hand down his pants:
Amanda said, "Oh don't mind him.
He's just feeling his oaths."

But wit won't flow so readily when the oath
involved is the one Amanda and Paul took seven years ago.
Its breaking was heard through their circle of friends
like the sharp crack of an ice-weighted branch:
a mile away, a dozen miles away or more, and still you know
what news the air has delivered. In fact I was out
of the country altogether, and yet—by one means
or another—I couldn't avoid reportage
of his drunken, nearly-falling-off-the-parapet declamations
on the roof of the Lattimore Building; or her being found
in a scrimmage of leaves and brushwood, where she'd spent the night
curled up and quiet and pale like some new-born creature
deposited there from another world. These two divorcing
examples of the enormity of a riven pledge.

How many promises, scattered to the winds
that were the province of the wind gods
of the Hopi, Blackfeet, Navajo, Cheyenne?
The Sioux. The Arapaho. The Algonquin.
How many hands were shook and names were signed
and pipes were passed congenially in a circle,
before the first of the used-car dealerships rose up
on ground where the gods had walked?
Not that the tribes had always dealt more honestly
with each other. (The very nature of a "trickster tale"

is—although it may ultimately be comic in effect—
deception.) God displays His covenant
with Noah by a rainbow . . . surely the grandest
signature ever! And a flight of birds for a fillip below.
But who would *want* to enter into contractual agreement
with a Being who could have concocted the Flood?
The Bible is silent on all of the hellish rot
that would have been revealed once the waters receded.
A planet of infants' skulls, and whatever is rendered
of flesh after forty days in the oceans.

What did we say to the oil-bearing nations?
What did they say in return, for a gun,
for an antibiotic, for a slice of processed cheese?
Some pledges, of course, are kept; my parents
made theirs under the *chuppa* and kept it alive
for as long as they were alive. But others . . . a girl
on the news, in a land I've never been to,
with a face that's marked by falling stone
from enemy fire. We're either the girl
or the enemy: this war is too confusing to know
such details as the lines of culpability.
Oaths of butter, oaths of mildew, of steel,
of putrefied skin, of juju bones, of shadow, of uranium,
oaths of gravel.

A Weather

Joseph Brodsky wrote a poem every year at
Christmas; more poets might adopt a holiday,
preferably an obscure one like Liberty Tree
Day or National Mustard Day.

— William Logan

That year I entered many clouds, and one,
the priestess cloud of them all, was more than darkness
—darkness, after all, is a static state—but
was an actively obliterative darkness: hungry, lurking
bushwhack darkness, on the prowl, the sasquatch,
the sachem, the badass savant of them all, a cloud
to surround a man like an all-devouring insect
after it mates, a kayo punch, a chemical dissolvent,
an empire darkness with its sneaky filamental darkness
colonizing the mind, and this was the overpowering culmination
that followed the cloud of unknowing, the cloud
of grovel, of deceit, of a ponderous umbrage—such
a year of inimical weather!—and so you can imagine
(and I invite you to do that very thing now) what it was like,
at last, on a stopover day in a tucked-away Bavarian village
when, with an hour to kill, I was given the tour
of an old-world circle of shingled buildings
where it was condimentally processed, and I entered one, the one
    in which
the troughs of seeds were ground to an airy golden dust,
and it was like walking into a golden cloud, a cloud
of light and of the kind of dust that light will become
on the last day of the universe, it coated me
and damascened my skin, it prickled a livening moisture
into the sorry deadwood of my eyes, and on my tongue
the ghosts of bitterroot and thorn were now replaced by this
revivifying tang of golden motion, I felt
liberated—newly leafed, newly fit for the arbor again—

and what did I long for, what did I dream?
—a sharp thin dribbled trail of it,
even from the dollar store,
even above the coals of the pit,
even in the cheap seats as the bodies slide into home.

Before Refrigeration

The sawdust, if laid on thickly, could be used
as insulation; and so in that way,
if they remained in the unlit cool of the hold
for the voyage, and were unloaded before the sun was up,
and stored—before their pickup by the customer—
in a shaded warehouse facing west,
the rough ton blocks of ice imported from Greenland
would survive their journey to London intact,
and be ready for use in the restaurant trade.
Once I wouldn't have had to explain this;

it was common knowledge. I wouldn't have had
to explain to my students
a pessary; a carpetbagger;
a buttonhook; carbon paper; sex
without the specter of AIDS; the Axis powers;
a naphtha lamp; a suffragette. And,
to be fair, the things that they've explained
to me—what emo is, and ska, and many-hundred
cyberwonderments—have disappeared the day
that they've been uttered. This afternoon I saw,

or thought I saw, an assemblage of objects
abandoned at the docks, that still (and I won't attempt
to persuade *your* sensibility) have, for me,
a lingering aura of fondness: standard neighborhood
mailboxes; a gather of corner telephone booths;
card catalogue cases . . . all of them, carved
from ice. There were enough for a village.
It *was* a village, of beautiful shapes in blue-white
that the sun was pleased to enter,
with only a touch of the melt first showing.

2008

"A Toast!"

to the newlyweds, Zach high-fiving,
Gwendolyn cupping her goblet of wine
as if—an obvious dearness—it's an infant's head
she plans on smooching, and Dillon
our resident realist/caustic opining
his usual "If you lived in Philly
you'd marry your one-true-only love and
if you lived in Seattle or Omaha you'd marry
your one-true-only love, so what
do 'one' and 'only' mean, or even
the idea of 'love'?"—not that
he can dampen this merriment, or the wonder

inherent in chance: we have five fingers on each hand
because amphibians had five digits, not because
that number is optimal for the human grasp. We
could have been otherwise-digited. We could
have been the lottery winner in Omaha,
besotted on luck and lucre, counting
luxury sedans o'erleaping stiles in dreams.
We could have been that corpse in Seattle,
discovered in a trunk at the wharf, its face
. . . well, you don't want to know,
believe me. Or in any case believe whoever
I am in this one of the multiplex

of existences. Some physics says that every time
we think "Well, but . . ." we fructify
a one-next-step (or one-step-less)
dimension. Let's admit it: there are half-tone lights
and shadow states of consciousness in which we've turned
a corner and entered a tangent world;
or turned in bed and she (or he
or you, yourself) were, in a ghostly fingersnap,

opaque to understanding. If you lived in Philly. . . .
If you lived in an exo-neural hologram body
under the moons of Mars. . . . *Well, but . . .*
and then that shift in the paradigm. I'll

admit it: there was a night I walked,
I walked, at an unknown moment I walked
through the tissue of atoms between two realms.
Who was I, here? Monsignor, swee' thang,
circus clown affixing his putty nose. . . .
Who was I *anywhere?* And who were these people
I said I loved, who said it back, revising
themselves each morning? I walked, I saw
a house, I looked in a window: a wedding scene:
"A toast!" And Zach high-sevens his guests,
and Gwendolyn makes a motherly nest
of all fourteen fingers around her wine.

A Partial List of Unacknowledged Musics
(Feel Free to Add Your Own)

And I think of the way that, say, an *a* or *e* exists
in written Hebrew: tiny dots or bars
below the consonants. As if the sex
or the grieved breath or the small flushed quail
of childish delight is only under
the floorboards of sturdier sounds. It could be
that's what we are: we're the vowels
set below the Music of the Spheres. We say
what their indifferent grandeur up in the heavens
can't. In the middle of the night, and in sight of the empyrean,
we're little, and low:
the human part.

．．

Who knows what music could be?
"Ten minutes" might be music
on the surface of Venus or Jupiter, it's so wacky
an idea there, where there *aren't* "minutes."
What a new way of seeing!
The travel of blood through the furls in the brain
or through an ear itself—that clef
attached to our head—has, obviously,
sound, although we'll never know
(it's like what "pleasure" is
in a partner) how this swells and diminishes and builds
and builds, orchestrally.

．．

At the première of *The Rite of Spring* in 1913,
audience reaction was so crazed and raucous
(some in cheering support, and others
histrionically booing this new—this dissonant,

indecorous—ballet) that, with the catcalls
of derision and the moans of an instantaneous pleasure,
not to mention the cane fights and umbrella brawls
that bristled up among these various factions . . . the dancers
moved "in time to music they had to imagine
they heard." / Once I saw a friend in a bar, in a sea
of heavy-metal-rock cacophony-uproar, silently reading
the sonnets of Edna St. Vincent Millay.

· ·

Who sang it originally? Rod Stewart,
I think. And then some female vocalist
did a cover version. But it was purely
an instrumental version I heard in the waiting room,
without having heard it, not consciously;
the hands inside my head that hold things up
for my attention were already overfull
and so didn't have room for that anthem
of early love gone wrong, "The First Cut
Is the Deepest." And then they arrived with the gurney
and wheeled me in to the deep well of sedation
where the prostate biopsy waited.

· ·

"Once, traveling in Argentina, he would insist
on sitting on every equestrian statue
in Buenos Aires." (Rachel Cohen, on Robert Lowell.)
I suspect there must have been a rousing martial music
playing in his brain the entire time, that no one heard,
but that was real for him, that heightened, even
validated, this manic, gloryful quest.
Somebody else might be astride a piece of driftwood

on the beach, and she would have—as don't we all?—
her own interior theme. "The flamingos are all dead,"
Bob once said to me. A *capital* "F," in *his* head,
where his love for that doo-wop group stays alive.

· ·

You're making love. You're making love, and
you aren't aware of anything outside of that lifting up
of the flesh into wings and sweet, sweet fire.
Or you're driving to the funeral, this first time
that you understand how grief inside your body
is also a turbulent river that floats your body.
And so it might be years, it might be ten years, more,
before some piped-in elevator music brings you back there,
where it also was, this music, whether you knew it or not.
That's how it was with the biopsy: one day, suddenly,
Duet for Knife and Blood rose up whole-force
from its unnatural slumber and haunted the land.

· ·

I've seen a stripper finish her set so sweated
with exuberance and otherworldly energy, her skin
in the lights looked coated over with diamond dust.
I've heard church choirs sing a sound that took them
off the ground as surely as 747 engine-roar.
Ah—but the wail of the seven-year-old daughter
in the burn ward . . . the staccato pop of gang guns
on the corner? Who knows *what* full range is needed
for a music that pleases the gods? All we can do
is hit what seem the proper notes. All we can do is make
a pleasing composition out of randomness
—as we are, for our while.

Countries

We must conclude that the birds [of isolated islands], not
having as yet learnt man is dangerous, disregard us [and are
therefore effortless to kill]. Pernety states that the Funarius
would almost perch on his finger. [Even so,] by Pernety's
account it was impossible to kill the black-necked swan. It is
rather an interesting fact, that this is a bird of passage, and
therefore brings with it the wisdom learned in foreign countries.

— arranged from Darwin, *Voyage of the Beagle*

1. Paying Her

And then her uncle who wasn't her uncle dragged her
into the shed and left a welt on her ass that turned
a dozen colors of sick. And then her daddy who wasn't
her daddy the same, or worse, or whatever. And then
her mother locked her out. And she and her brother ate
what was left on the bones. And so she learned
to think around a corner, and to have a story tricking on her tongue
for any hustler-, sap- or asshole-of-the-moment.
And then the military. The pregnancy. The six months
living with both kids in the car ("We washed
with cups of water from out of the Kwik Trip"). Stripping.
Saving. And then the four-star penthouse apartment and
then the fucker who gutted her account and then
and then and then. And so she learned in her life
as a ho to play the straights like trout on a line and
what was up and what was cool and what was hot
and what was so way hella hot the street kings even
weren't down with that number. And so to look at her now,
age 30, in her glitter and slink that dominate
a room, is to witness a culminant body
of traits best fit to succeed in their socio-niche.
I can't imagine him, so inward and prissy, sitting in a room
with Smoke (her sometimes name): I can't imagine

the two of them on the same *planet*. And yet they
have been, along with the finches, slugs and tortoises
he studied, and the Oxford dons and vicars
of his voluminous correspondence, along with my parents,
my friends, the ape of our common ancestry: he might
have politely ordered her a drink, and got
his notebook out, and paid her strict attention.

2. Eyes

It's Kansas: where, last year, the school board outlawed
evolution: so we feel indeed like outlaws
here on Nella's porch, the eight of us (with Huey
and his date still due in under an hour), reading
aloud from his *Beagle* text below a moon that would have
silvered, similarly fully, the Galápagos; and Tahiti;
and Tierra del Fuego, its mountain torrents and up-torn trees,
and even here, where "Death, instead of Life, seemed
the predominant spirit," they found "a snug little harbour"
and his entries continued unabated, the "swampy peat,"
the shellfish, the seals. . . . Sharing this in the heart
of the Kansas religiopolitical nexus, sensing
the incipient itch of his theory coming on, we feel almost
insurrectionist, which is silly of course when I really consider
these civil stay-in-the-speed-limit tax-paying cautionary
friends of mine. (He would have "fit right in"
with them, Introvert, Cerebral, Mister Stick-in-the-Mud Himself.)
And as we're trading favorite passages [Sharona offers
"The elegance of the grasses, the novelty of the parasitical plants. . . .
Delight is a weak term to express the feelings of a naturalist
who, for the first time, has been wandering by himself
in a Brazilian forest," and over our brie and chardonnay Yolanda
reads "They explained they wanted gifts of knives by acting
as if they had a piece of blubber in their mouth, and then
pretending to cut it"], Huey arrives at 8 p.m.
with his date, "Hey everybody, this is Sandi," at which
Smoke's eyes and mine don't meet to suggest that I've danced with her
in a gangsta bar while she was butt-naked
—very different circumstances;
almost different species.

3. Scram

the inhabitants of this country   *And then she leaped drunk*
onto a table, and then she pulled me up too and was grinding
her ass in my crotch to the ten-thousand decibel beat
and a skanky white bitch got in her face and started
talking fucking stupid mess   among these indigenes   *and one pimp*
had his heater out and was fucking shouting shit
their customs are relative   *and the po-po came*
with their sirens and flashers and she was in somebody's car
by then and screaming FUCK THE PO-LEECE FUCK
and their tasers were drawn   the rules of the tribe   *and*
then, and then.

              At 9 p.m. an officer approaches Nella's porch
for the innocent purpose of asking if anyone here had seen
a neighbor child's runaway pooch, just that, no more
than that: and yet I'm not surprised when we discover
only a few minutes later that "Sandi" has vanished
into the dark—"like smoke," somebody says, and Huey
confusedly and disconsolately picks it up for a mantra
through the rest of the night: "like smoke." I picture her
out there, somewhere, hair a wild tangle of the same
smooth silver moonlight that, in the back room, lends
a courtly and heraldic look to Nella's seven-year-old daughter
practicing violin. "But *why* did she just run off?"
Phil whines, as if some precious code he understands is broken and
another one threatens to take its place. I can't explain.
I know, but can't explain the overabundance of life in her,
its beauty and its bruises, and its self-protective savviness
that keeps a blinkless watch throughout the day.
But Darwin, I think, would recognize her shoulders lift
with the rush of the black-necked swan, that brings
a wisdom the world beat into it from far away.

The Severed Stone Head of Shiva's Wife,
and the Bionic Stripper, and Thoreau,
and the Cabin Boy in Tahiti,
and the Pearl Diver Ravished by Octopi
(and Others)

The Versions

The Spanish, under Quiroz o Torres, discovered,
and lay claim to, Tahiti late in the sixteenth century.
In 1767 an English expedition commanded by Samuel Wallis
claimed Tahiti for England. One year later
Louis-Antoine de Bougainville lay anchor there
and claimed Tahiti for France. The hall of history
says so. Next door, in the hall of art history,
X-ray shows a painting that began with an infant's head,
a loosely yolky thing. And painted over that
was the face of a famous paramour-for-hire, pale
and gorgeously veined, like a fine dessert cheese.
Over that, the head of the regent. There are always,
it seems, conflicting founding stories. Under this poem:
another poem, a mind-your-own-damn-business poem

· ·

too naked—let's say yolky—for its own good;
then it became an attempt to say its concerns
through summarizing Bougainville's Tahitian voyage
(although the French had christened the island "La Nouvelle Cythère,"
the New Island of Love) . . . but that poem died—a compost—
into this one. In the hall of human anomalies, we see
the X-ray of Gian-Giacomo Libbera: a dwarfish twin,
all waist-to-toes, dangles out of his abdomen, with
its primitive head *inside* Libbera's body, attached
to his rib cage . . . call it a rough draft, call it a botched
alternative genome, of this man who went on to marry
"and have four children, and lead an active social life."
Of course the hall of human development reminds us
of the gill-thing and the tufted-thing and the pelted-thing

· ·

we all were, on our uterine way here. On the way
to Tahiti, at some point Bougainville would have realized
his botanist Commerson's "cabin boy" was Commerson's
mistress smuggled aboard in disguise. We don't know
what delight or suffering was hers, but in some version
of this poem, we see her alone one night at the rail
sighing so heavily into the ocean air it might be both
of her selves relieving some great emotional weight
at once. She's gorgeous—of course. She's a handful
of spitfire minx—of course. The waters are gorgeous too,
and prone to mercurial moods. Right now
they're silverfoiled by the moon. A full moon . . . look,
it has a face inside, of the loveliest lavender
features, partly covered but recognizable still.

Return Suite: The Little Click

A ninth-century Cambodian statue of a wife of the Hindu god Shiva was decapitated in the fifteenth century, and the head and its torso were lost to each other for six hundred years—until May 9, 2006, when, through chance, they both wound up at the same museum. "I heard the little click you get when two stones fit together, and the head fell perfectly into place. It was as if it had put itself together. I still get goose-bumps thinking about it."

– from coverage in Fortean Times

1.

It wasn't with the apocalyptic crack of what would later be "Africa"
yawing away—soil, leaf, and lake—from what would later
be "South America." Still, as splits go, it was dramatic enough;
and one night Jill was discovered with his name in her throat
and her hand on a knife; and one day Ray was found with a whore
he'd dressed up in Jill's clothing; and the lawyers,
meanwhile, practiced their usual banditry. Nor did it partake
—or anyway, not mostly—of the special tarantella
that so eerily remembers various pleasures and desperations
across an amputee's stump; and even so, by the difficult cramp
that had entered her formerly yoga-perfect posture,
by the look of extra-gees that so frequently squeezed his face
as if he were training in astronaut camp . . . we understood
that each of them carried around a "phantom life" that hurt
the nub left over from parting. On their final night
in the house together they were as dead to one another as Arthur
is supposedly dead in the coffin made of hollowed-out oak
and buried in the churchyard of St. Dunstan, never again
to lift the weight of Excalibur over his head
or feel the slippery cinch of Guinevere easing herself on the rise of him
—and Barbarossa, dead; and Jesus; and Quetzalcoatl; and Gilgamesh.

And yet all of those myths, and hundreds of others, assume
the possibility that some residual spritzle of electrolytes,
some thread (it worked for Theseus), *some* version
of effectuating need and an agency fit to its viable implementation
allows a return.

2.

Renunciation: no longer a nun.
Good-bye to the Lenten fare and celibacy and matins, there
on the pier as her little solo rowboat huffs out into the adventuresome
    waters!
Yes, but in her memoir she reveals how the orderliness
and sacrifice of that earlier existence reappear with a tenacity
she'd never have guessed at back in the cloister; sometimes, still,
she's had the Blessed Virgin speak a quiet word of doom or consolation
through Big Tits Girl at the beauty shop, with the smell of a perm in
    tremulous waves
surrounding her like incense . . . a theology
correlative, she posits, to the neurosensory ghost dance
of the amputee. It seems no matter how necessary
the surgery, we yearn toward reattachment.
So the vestige wants the primacy again.
So a bee is only the leading edge of a path
that goes back to the hive.
The broken alloy wants its subatomic hinge again.
The mother is held from leaping into her daughter's open grave.
The light loves being light; the vapor would never forfeit
its mizzly solitude in the air; and yet they each sigh, in their own way,
when they remember their moment of rainbow.
There is a gravity, a working inner orrery, that keeps a heron
coming back to the same bend of this river every year:
the glow at sunset is a rapprochement
between the bird and the water. Distance
is always forgiven: Cinderella's foot might well have carried her
to Shanghai in the interim, to Mars,
but the slipper of glass will never shun their reuniting.

3.

Sometimes the return is in a covert guise. (Odysseus entering Ithaka.)
It was half-a-century back that I was a child guided
brusquely through a museum display to see the mallet-dented gold
of Agamemnon's face-plate . . . here it is today, as the skin
of a large smoked kipper.

        Thus do Jill and Ray
return to the poem—as other people. In fact
as their own lawyers,

                who have seen so much, for so long, of their clients'
riven hearts, that each is also, in his/her own way,
considering divorce. For Ruth, this means an efficient
divvying-up in her mind of who-gets-what before the first
attempt at arbitration. Okay. But for Oliver,
who's witnessed the underground lode of potential fire
in Ray—a vast, compacted bituminous range within him,
awaiting the pickaxe, awaiting the match—it means
on alternating days he's moved to "make it work," to love Vonelle
in those passionate declarations we associate with an aria.
And Vonelle . . . ?—is a technician in the Indian Subcontinent department
of the museum I mentioned up in line 3, assigned to labor all week
in an annex room of statuary fragments—miscellania,
a jumble of cultures and centuries—to make sense
of these unconnected puzzle-parts, if there's sense to be made.
Through Thursday, into Friday, she's been trapped in this
fluorescent box of severance and stone dust,
utterly flummoxed, and then, with only an hour left
(and she's so excited at this, she bursts it out
to Oliver as soon as he gets home, although "to be honest"
"it's not as if," "you know," "things are going so well"
between them), "Something . . ."—what? We'll never hear it,
since he's fresh from a frightening bout of rayandjillitude,

130

and squeezes Vonelle as if she might inflate for him
into a life preserver designed to carry them
over their current rift, their current disastrous marital
plate tectonics, and everything after "Something . . ." must be
sacrificed to that, here, where we leave them
to randy around all night in this incomplete third section.

4.

Orchidectomy: (from Latin *orchis,* "orchid";
from Greek, "testicles"; akin to Middle Irish *uirgge,* "testicle"),
the process of creating a castrato: "In Italy,
during the seventeenth and eighteenth centuries, up to 4,000 boys
    were castrated
annually." Normally he was between the ages of eight and ten,
anesthetized with opium first, and set in a bath of milk
(to soften the genitals) or a tub of chill water (to numb him
and limit the bleeding): then the cut would be made
in his groin, and his spermatic cord and testicles fished out
of their slippery nest and flung to the pigs. The price
in freakishness was high, but the successful
of these singers (one in a hundred, probably) wound up
enormously famous, showered in flowers
after every performance, and wealthy. Theirs were voices
that floated above all others—holy oil
on top of the common waters. Still,
Domenica Mustafa (whose long-past childhood operation and its reasons
were a blur to him) is reported to have grabbed a knife
at a dinner party, exclaiming, "If I learned tonight
that it was my father who ordered this, I should open
his throat!" We can only guess crazily at the dream-lives
of these part-men. Talk about "phantom limb"!
Ours is just conjecture, of what succubi
and ache flew through those twisted nights, to land inside
the sexual amnesia. But we do know this: our human urge
is always toward the missing; "In some parts of England
it is said yet that Arthur is not dead,
but he shall come again among us when he is most needed." At night
in the menstrual hut, the woman fasts and prays aloud that her vessel,
which has been emptied, will be full again. (And it is.) Outside,
the people pray to the waned moon, that it begins again

to accrete itself into wholeness. (And it does.)
If the electrically jangling cut-edge of the amputee is our trope,
does that make every observant Jew a nerve-end
sensitive to the Lost Tribes of Israel?—ten
of an original twelve ("only the tribes of Benjamin and Judah
became the ancestors of the modern Jews"). How likely is it,
once they titrate into the general bloodstream of the species,
that they'll resolidify out of it some day, bearing their shields,
chanting from the scrolls of their priesthoods . . . entities again?
Not very. And still the theories (the British, the Malaysians,
you-name-it) abound. The dreams of recovery forever abound.
The night air of the seventeenth and eighteenth centuries might have been
invisibly filled with flocks of those "orchids,"
homeless now, perpetually afloat, and mewling overhead
for the carnal roots from which they were removed . . . a sound
that keeps their populations of emasculated singers
awake until sunrise, in torment and hope.
                                    In Niklaus Manuel's
The Execution of John the Baptist (1517), the decapitator
—dressed in the stylish pleats and trimwork
of a Swiss mercenary soldier—holds the head by its beard
as casually as a seasoned chef might shake a lettuce
to drain it while he's thinking of a dozen different things.
He's more intent on the silver platter he receives
(with a little flourishful bow) in his other hand
from Salome, whose eyes are lidded and make her look
unnervingly blasé. The head shows more emotion
than either of them. And the two men who carry the body away
on a stretcher are clearly in a rush (we only see a boot
of the one in the lead, he's so out of the frame already) as if afraid
some vital alchemical sympathy of attraction might,
even now, with the puddle of blood still trembling, sexualize
the air and kiss his two parts back together.

5. The Head of Shiva's Wife
(and Quoting Two Words from Vonelle)

Once I was part of a system—as was Pluto,
one more round stone unconnected now
to its earlier body. Demoted. And, while any dislocation
has a claim to pain, I'll say that mine occurred across
those special inner knuckles where the voice is born
of breath and its constraint; and where the heart
in its wildest speculation is said
to leap; and the sour wad of revulsion,
the same; and where the tour of love's tongue
through a skin's most arousable excitation-nooks
so often begins, with easy access up
to the ear and down to the breast. And so I lay
my little claim to a particular discomfiture.
I waited over centuries in a place
that was no place at all—a nullity
outside of viability and touch. I wanted my Shiva again.
I wanted my own proud nipples again,
and the shoulders with which the dance would double
the energies and precisions of my feet. I wanted simply
what you want: what you so ordinarily have: but I
no longer bore even a heart with which
to feel the striking pang of my own absence. Even so,
I came closer—a grain at a time, a grain of time
at a time. A speck. I wept. A dot. I sorely lamented,
beyond consolation. A nodule. A microscopic
constellation of nodules. I waited. I wailed
inside the weight of my stone brain. Then, one day,
the Joy took place. I heard a woman's voice
exulting—or, to be more accurate, I heard it
as if I read her mind—and from across the cosmic darkness
lit by sporadic magnesium flares, I flew,
I returned, I was one with the One. "Something . . ."
and I became immanent ". . . clicked."

That Was the Year

"Man's life is but seventy salads long."
— Ralph Waldo Emerson

of the salad of aluminum foil and iron filings.
Then the year of the salad of hope in a cool sauce
sweetened with mother's milk and topped
with the plumage of chimney storks. And after that,
a slaw of remaindered books. Then next, the year
of mysalad.com. So many. Some, you've barely
nibbled at. Others, you've grabbed in your hands
and swallowed in swinish glee. It comes
from "salt"; who *doesn't* come from salt, as witness
the tear, and the laboring brow, and the tang
of our sexual broths. The dictionary also says
"an incongruent mixture: HODGEPODGE." *That's*
familiar, here, age sixty; every day a little
too much to digest; too old to turn over a new leaf.

• •

These are true: Gangarum Gautum, of Kanpur, India
"started eating grass secretly when he was seven";
now at 41 he claims "to have eaten nothing
but grass for the last five years." In a village
in India, neighbors of a woman named Bangari
"have given up hanging out their wash to dry": she's
"hooked on a diet of cotton clothes," having begun
"as a toddler." Pest controller Zhong Zhisheng
of Shaoguan City, China specializes in ridding houses
"of wasps, that he takes home and cooks in light oil."
I have colleagues who have eaten administrative
shit for decades now. Thoreau and his legendary two years
of beans, beans, beans, beans, beans. A couple leaving
a motel: their mouths in a smileful satiation.

• •

The salad of basilisk and wyvern meats.
The famous nothing salad: auger holes
and black holes, with the zeroes out of a Swiss cheese.
There are so many I could invent, but they
would all stand for the real and everyday:
tossed, garden, spring mix, tuna, Caesar,
ham, egg, Waldorf, Asian medley, cobb,
the one with kiwi fruit, the one with knobs of radish. . . .
Seventy: that's *a lot* of salads!—until the last
is in sight, and then who *wouldn't* eat the salad of sand
if necessary, the salad of burr and rue; for even regret
is a flavor, and better even boredom on the tongue
than not to have a tongue. Heaven is a pretty theory,
so long as the smorgasbord table is full.

· ·

In his study, in the clear light of a Concord
afternoon, Ralph Waldo Emerson is committing a thought
to paper for an essay, and his unexpected visitor
must wait for those few minutes in an anteroom
until the thought is as clear as the light. Thoreau
understands; he isn't miffed. If anybody's irked here
it's the host, whose concentration—*there!*
again!—is ruined repeatedly by what he's come
to recognize are not the creaks of floorboards, but
a flatulence abundantly admitted from his guest
in punctuation. Still, the essay being dabbed at *is*
his (now canonical) "Friendship." He smiles. . . .
Life is too brief for harboring ire.
To every man, his salad.

Unseen

"Up to his day, Japanese artists had never
drawn clouds, only mists."
— Paul Johnson on Hokusai

Not that it never rained in Japan.
It rained, and sometimes hard—the wind could whip it
into your face with the force of a sodden *obi*. Other
times, a lightly pecking shower down your neck:
the horses never acknowledge it, although
some flowers just the size of *sake* cups retain
the liquid proof. So did their artists
never look up toward the source of this,
for *centuries*? the farmers in their paddies
and the soothsayers . . . surely *they*
consulted those astounding metamorphic floating silos
of the waters of earth! And surely they had names . . .
a fleeting child's-purse of water . . . a fortress. . . .
Hokusai's erotic print of the woman, a pearl diver,
being pleasured by two exploring octopi . . . she's
on her back, and surely in the moments just before
this rousing interspecies slithermix of tissues
she'd have been aware of sky that,
in her youth, with a friend, in some rare lull
between the day's imperatives, they'd fill with the usual
fancies: like an otter, like a lotus, like a boy's you-know. . . .
Or is it that their artists simply *chose*
the mist to the actual mysterious, dangerous holding-place
of our sustenance and storms? The way we sometimes choose
the sobbing, and the weaving scarves of laughter
on the night—the fore, the after—to the difficulty
of love itself. Perhaps they trusted delicacy,
and believed that implication sufficed.
The hem says the kimono.

• •

137

He was also the first in Japan "to learn
to draw shadows" and to understand the seascape
"as a subject in its own right." What
we don't see! In the West—at least so goes
the standard storyline—a mountain was just an impediment
in the arts, as in life, until Petrarch made his climb
in the fourteenth century; and even so it isn't until about
the eighteenth century that a mountain is truly *seen*
(with moods, and character, in the way that the coast
and the forests had opened up their individual
sublimities and terrors: their faces) and Kenneth Clark,
the critic, says that "to Erasmus, Montaigne, Descartes, Newton,
practically any of the great civilisers I have mentioned,
the thought of climbing a mountain for pleasure
would have seemed ridiculous." This, while their counterpart
artists in Japan were recording the magisterial, corrugated
ranges of that island with an attentive fidelity
sensitive to the travel of light as it modulates
the mineral surface, and empathetic to every stubby
roothold in a wrinkle of stone. Talk about
"cultural relativism." What we don't see! The ultraviolet
mazes that the bee meanders, we clodhopper
blindly through. A girl, alone, on break between
the enervating dives for pearls, is casually squatting
on a shingle of rock, immersed in conversation
with her invisible friend, who loyally accompanies her
all day . . . "alone" is only a word
for the limit of my perception. Or a man considers
a woman in their bed, as she sleeps, as a scraggle
of ruby-highlight jet hair zigs across her forehead. . . .
Well, he knows what he's like. So why does she stay
with him, *what* does she see in him that he doesn't
see in himself? It's nuts: we've mapped so much
by now of the red-tumeric sands and screes
of Mars, its rifts and crinkles

are forever in the bytes of our computerware with an accuracy
most family photo albums only dream of, we've observed
the thousand-mile spumes of dust storms at its polar caps,
and the moon? . . . the moon! . . . by now we've seen
the diadems cratered into its earthward presence
with the 20/20 focus of ideal, detailed sight . . . and yet
he'll never see what *she* sees
under the petals of her eyelids as they ride
on the pools of her dreaming.

• •

An experiment: the subjects view a video
of a basketball game, under the instruction to keep their eyes
on the ball-in-motion . . . and a girl in a gorilla costume
at one point walks across the court. Of course
the results are no surprise to us,
who know that even as the shrewdest minds in Europe
carriage past the rising foothills of some mountain chain
without a halt,
                Hokusai was at work on his series
One Hundred Views of Mt. Fuji. What a joy
it would have been, to watch *his* joy, as he added
shadows!—under a tilting group of wine-imbibers,
enormously in the wake of oxen, subtly below the irises,
or dropped from their bodies like eggs
as the startled waterfowl take to the air. . . . In addition
to woodblock prints and painting that left his hands
in a copious flow (and he labored on, productively,
through his eighty-ninth year), his fifteen books
of "random sketches" (*manga*: we inherit
his word) hold over 40,000 drawings: rumples in a tossed-off cloth,
the foam of a wave, an eagle in a blizzard,
bridges, an elephant, the shogun's warriors, ghosts,
more bridges, a tiger roaring, a woodcutter and his axe,

the shape of a dragon in volcano smoke, the elaborate hair
of ladies of the court, the moon on snow, the look of moist
and parted thighs, a woodcutter smoking a pipe,
more bridges still . . .
                              the pleasure
every day of seeing, always finer,
always more precisely, and so therefore seeing as if
for the original time, where there hadn't been seeing
previously. . . . "80 percent of the subjects
said that they saw 'nothing unusual'
take place there on the basketball court."

                              • •

After her day of rigorous labor diving
off the shelfrock for her basketworth of pearls
—exhilarating at times, and brilliantly lithe,
but rigorous—she comes home to her pallet with a weariness
that can only be prelude to sleep. . . . Right now I
don't want to argue gender politics, yak yak yak. The fact is
the female sexual organ is "negative space"
in terms of visual imaging. And if ever there's someone
who needs for his drawings to fill a vacuum,
it's Hokusai. In *The Dream of the Fisherman's Wife*
he has the larger octopus's mouth so gluily attached
to her own sweetly tart receiving-damp, they're one
continuous pulse. Its arms festoon her naked body
with the gift of all-over sensual tease (one coil
dollops a nipple). And a smaller octopus offers itself
to her mouth—her head is thrown back and her eyes closed
and there isn't an inch of her self not given over
gladly to rapture. It was, at that time, "one of the rare attempts,
in either Asiatic or European art, to symbolize
sexual pleasure as it is experienced by the female."
So, again, we find him seeing what might not

have been seen without him. This is true in the West,
of Turner and industrial steam. Of Rothko
and the soulful seep of pure, abstracted color. In 1802
the Quaker Luke Howard wrote a paper that put forward
an attempted classification of clouds. He influenced painters
like Constable, who turned out hundreds of studies
of those unstudyable bodies, "noting on the back the month,
and time of day, and direction of the wind." We know his father
was a wine merchant; Ruskin said that Constable
"bottled clouds as carefully as his father bottled sherries."

• •

My friend Gisella is serious now (she's
talking about her therapy). She squares her shoulders,
puffs the errant strand of ruby-highlight jet hair
off her face, and continues explaining
how thankful she is; we all have inner tremor-lines
and monsters to confront, but never see them
on our own; and now a decade "under expert care"
has given her the insight and the fledgling courage
to recognize, and so begin to master,
the darks and the knottedness that she's been carrying
with her all her life. Because I like her, I wish her
a shield and sword, a gallant steed, a magic ring,
whatever it takes. "Does Stu know?"
"Albert, *no one* else can ever really *know.*"
She sets her jaw in a look we call "determination,"
and sets her eyes on . . . what? I try
to look there. . . . And then suddenly
I can see them too.
The mountain that she needs to face.
The cloud that always follows her.
The long persistent shadow.

The Story of Wax and Wane

Things change over time etc., a river
redoes the banks with even its most gentle of caresses
etc. Language too: "Infomercials,"
"crackho," "blogger," "particle accelerator"
bellying out of the matrix-slime
and testing the flex of their cilia
on the shore of a first appearance . . .

just as "devoir" and "caitiff" and "harrico"
return to that element, this time disappearing
in its more corrosive aspect. Once,
a "typewriter" was the person
behind the machine, and not the machine.
Once, we lit cigarettes with "lucifers."
In the fullness of time, the language

Middle Chulym has come to be spoken
by only 426 people—hunter-gatherers in Siberia,
"none of them under fifty-two." The wind, that old
absconder, snatches the words away as soon
as they're offered aloud, it drives down
out of that sky the color of sturgeon-leak,
it pockets "radish," it grinds "love" to a rosin,

it bends to the faces and it soul-kisses
sentences out of those mouths as whole and elastic
as eels. The wind, "the wind of time," it makes
our finest cerebration its own intellectual property,
it makes our songs about lust its own sexual chattel.
The wind. The ocean. The night. Vocabulary doesn't
stand a chance, in their digestion. Hamlet,

talktalktalktalktalktalktalk, soliloquizing
his agony into the sixteenth century Denmark air:
"fellies" he says, and "fardels" he says—*what???*—and the wind,
the Siberian wind, reduces this to spittlefleck: and then
to invisible pinches-worth of hydrogen and oxygen,
from these to mix the water in which
"cyclotron" is baptized, "dotcom," "zip-a-tone,"

"nerdy," "jewfro," "polyurethane." In the fullness.
In the passion of the river for the medium
it changes as it flows. In a picture I'm looking at
now, a woman sits behind an office typewriter
—it's a standard 1960s model, and so is she—
and indulges herself in a cigarette. The smoke
like a scarf she's fluttering. The picture, marinated in time.

. .

The engine-revving premise of *Then They Were Married*
—that astute, high-style comic strip
Cliff Sterrett created—is simple; and it must have provided
a mirror to its readers' lives they welcomed
as an accurate description: it repeated
its single joke over numerous years in the 1930s
and under alternative titles: *Belles—and Wedding Bells*;

Sweethearts—and Wives. You get the idea.
In the courtship stage, he'll keep a sturdy silence
(in a whirl of inky zigzag gashes stabbing at his stomach)
rather than ever imply the hammer-smash, unpalatable nature
of her salmon-jelly casserole: and on the other side
of the "Then They Were Married" panel, we see him fling
a chafing-dish out the window as if it's a fuming Bolshevik bomb.

His snoring, the same . . . her outlandish galoshes . . . his sharp
    whiskers . . .
it will all be cherished, all be damp
and saccharine in lovergoo, as it will also be
little lumps in graves to piss on. In the mineral eyes
of mica and coal a geologic era watches with,
it will all occur, the whole abobble bouillabaisse.
A war—or not "a" war, but the current

visible edge of a continuous condition. Then a breath
—a day; a generation; a featherfall—of peace. A rose,
let's say a rose at its peak, a great symphonic rose.
And then its petals scattering like unconnected notes. *Sex,
intellection, fidelity, boredom, betrayal, apology, sex again*—a wheel.
The fullness of time demands it.
The narrative needs of a story demand it.

                          • •

And so the couple enters this poem—*re-enters,*
for they were here all along. The secretary,
over her typewriter keyboard with the cocked wrists
of a pianist; the suave and exotic go-getter guy
from a village east of Chulym (via apprenticeship
on the floor of the London Stock Exchange): against
that drab background of global ever-war,

he's given her those roses. Now they're on the wheel,
fifteen years of man-and-woman wheel. Maybe
we know them. Maybe there's something, oh,
familiar when he's in the room with her and more alone
than when he's by himself. She used to be . . .
well, anyway, she's not. She's all involved now in her "art"
with her "artist friends." "You just don't get it,"

she lectured him once, "it's leaves and sand
intentionally, it's *supposed* to decompose." He drove out,
one afternoon, without her, to view it. An "eco-installation."
Even as he watched, it seemed to slightly curl and rustle
in the increasing chill of the season, it heaved
and darkened—it became something else.
He got it. When my friend Michael Pointer

was six, an uncle gave him a watch from the 1930s
that had two radium-painted hands. "Turn off the lights.
See? Glows in the dark!" It took a year
for Michael to figure out the mysterious burn
on his wrists, a deepening raw sienna.
He'd been altered every hour
by the sear of one more circle.

                                    • •

And then the Earth will be jacketed in ice. And then
the Earth will be a furnace of baking jungle terrain.
Everything—in the fullness; in the photon eyes of the stars.
And us? . . . we'll float on serotonin highs, we'll sink
in the greedy mulch of despair. . . . There's a word for this.
Bipolar.
Why should we be any different than the planet?

                                    • •

"Software." "Cyborg." "Morning-after pill."
In order for these and their kin to wriggle for the first time
into the sun and dry their just-sprung wings,
other words must clamber backwards
and drown. "Postilion." "Thimblerigger." "Mugwumppery."

They drown, they're dead forever; or they drown
and are reborn, sometimes in bodies that are stranger

than they could ever imagine. So when Hamlet
and his enemies and friends at castle Elsinore
address us in their grandiose suffusions,
while the spirit of it is eternal, the spoken skin
is as susceptible to a sloughing-away as any,
"stithy," "mazzard," "quillets," "cataplasm,"
and some words over the centuries have reversed

their polarity altogether. "Season your admiration,"
says Horatio, "season" meaning not "add flavor to,"
but "tone down." Or "I'll make a ghost of him
that lets me"—I would think that "lets" here means
"allows," but it means "hinders." In an early scene,
when Hamlet is informed of his father's spectral presence,
and all of the tragedy's dominoes are first arranging themselves

along those cold and stony battlements, he says,
"Would I had met my dearest foe in heaven
As ever I had seen that day," and "dearest" here
means "bitterest." Who might have guessed
that even the fullness of time would occasion a shift like that?
(And so the couple re-enters this poem.)
You heard me: "dearest" was "bitterest."

Linear

Once, a world where animals, all animals,
were wild. Then eventually the concept of "pet."
I'd guess, said Jen, the line between those two occurs
at approximately the same time as the line between the forest or jungle
and "lawn." Sounds right. Especially if "approximately"
or "circa": ways we engineer some wiggle-room
into otherwise inflexible demarcations. There are lines
like these that slice across the walkways of our lives
by the bajillion, invisibly. Who knows (any more than did
the fish that clambered onto land or, turning back,
the land beast that reverted to a whale) when we've crossed some
evolutionary line?—it's not like a tripwire
setting off automatic confetti and horns, and yet
a line, by any definition, should be drawable enough.
Between the zygote and the next stage up. Between the side
of the girlie club with G-strings and the side with total nudity.
In her crazyass sexed-up heyday Jen was a dancer.
Then eventually the concept of "wife." For seven years
she worked at that: and still one night walked back out
to her earlier life where wide-eyed men with dollar tips lined up for her.

It's 99° and the air is as still as a picture of air,
our bodies are heavy, inescapable enclosures —solid
masses of discomfort—as under other conditions
they can be solid containers of stroked-skin pleasure.
On the quantum level . . . spectral subsubparticles exist
in "here" and "here-prime," are entangled (not in "time")
with subsubparticle-kin in dozens of places at once,
if "place" and "once" have any meaning we can fathom,
and they don't. What does it mean, to be the sum of this
surreal indeterminacy, and where's the line between
the rules of human life . . . and the rules of that life's
quantum mechanical elements? *Is this confused gray area why*
psychosis exists? Is this why ghosts exist? or gods? or why
we hurt each other? Is this why a mother who drunkenly yelled to the world
from a rooftop's edge *I Hate My Daughter!* sobs now
at that daughter's hospital bedside?—now that the accident
sheared off an arm. Sobbing, crooning, all night
lullabying: what the French once thought to call *chantpleure,*
"to sing *and* weep at the same time." Yes; so much
of what we feel uses us up on both sides of the line.

It happened so quickly!—her shift was done, she left
The Wiggle Room absorbed in counting a green, green roll of ones,
some shit-head after-curfew teenage driver squeal-wheeled
around the corner, and . . . a year and four months later, Jen
is increasingly deft in the use of her experimental
bionic arm: its twenty micro-motors and a hustling constellation
of computer chips are married to the phantom arm
her mind still holds intact. It seems a natural extension
of her lithe, ambrosial body. Sy she calls it (last name
Borg) or Anne (for Droid), and someday everyone may be a place
where bio- and electro- zizzle back and forth across what used to be
a wall between, and whether A) you loathe or B) you dive
like an animatronic porpoise expectantly into that future says
a huge amount of who you are and with what comfy ease or friction
you'll be heading there. Today it's 99°, and you should see her
wipe her forehead free of sweat—like anybody! "Look,
I've practiced"—inching down her jeans to show
a folded dollar bill in the pink side string of her thong,
which she extracts with the finesse of a proficient Oliver Twist.
"A year ago I couldn't draw a straight line."

He hadn't done a line of coke, or meth, or pot, or even
the watery beer that Dogboy always had in the trunk, but
neurological studies suggest that the decision-making capacity
of a teenage brain is only partially formed—the part,
for example, that calculates risk and foresees consequence.
And yet, of course, civilization was set on its path from *then*
to *us* by people who rarely lived out of their teenage years.
Is this why peace is always casting a shadow called war?
why truth has a thousand names on its birth certificate?
why we've come so far, to make the old gestures of pissing
on vows and thumping our chests and thinking the tender moments
will last forever? In any case, there was the triangle: him,
the car, and her crushed body. Guilt is a ferret, sleepless,
hungry for the meat in the heart: it won't stop chewing. As part
of his exoneration, the judge decreed he must visit her
after a year. And when he does so, any bad-boy truculence left in him
is on its knees in front of her suddenly—bawling like a baby.
And any resentment in her is washed away: she carefully
aligns her arm and his bent head, and gently strokes
his hairline in prosthetic benediction.

Between the clownfish and the thousand-tentacled, wriggling room
in which it lives—its anemone, "den and hiding place
and breeding ground and shielding surround of protection, so that
for its entire life the clownfish rarely strays beyond
a few yards from this center"—is a symbiotic line
of such exquisite calibration, such a perfect teeter-tottering
of porousness and separation, we (for all of our reef-marine biology
and our poetry) can pretty much do no more than be wonderstruck.
/ "Assimilation": Hungarian, tribal Blackfeet, Black, Latino, Jewish,
Vietnamese: and some Big Thing called "American" on the other repellant
or all-absorptive side of the line. / Between the ancestors, up
in the traditional Chinese "afterlife," and their descendants sending them
gifts of "grave money," burning bills that read "The Bank of Heaven,
Co., Ltd."—wow. / Between the secessionists' fervent bombs and
the Republic's counter-bombs: the line moves back and forth a mile or two
each week. / Between the dream and the day. / Between the sides
of the moon. / Between the idea of what we want
from the marriage, and what it does or doesn't supply. /
Between the barn and its shadow: in over a century,
neither of them has canceled one of their dates.

She was dead for a while—flat-lined—then a Doctor
Rhonda Hsu resparked her, into ongoingness.
Hsu comes from a pedigreed line of medical specialists, back
through generations of hill-land healer-visionaries. Jen's mother
comes from a line of assholes. (Stories of the brawls,
and the cops, and the fuckfriend-of-the-night would only grow tedious.)
"And you work like a whore, at that tittie bar"—like *she*
was a Sunday school paragon! At least Jen *worked!* etc.
But a near-death wreck, it turns out, in the end can serve to translate
even the most incomprehensible family angers, and I think
of the Rosetta Stone—how after a thousand failed attempts to crack
the millennial silence of the ancient Egyptian hieroglyphics, it
provided an occasion for the lines of separate languages
to talk to one another. On that first day out of ICU,
the frail voice of the one and the husky maternal voice of the other
entered dialogue across a decade's rift. And you could see them
do a careful conversationalist's tense version of a tightrope master's
step by step progression—tipping; in a flash
rebalancing; almost tipping again—along the line that, similarly,
because you're his, Johnny Cash says he walks.

If one believes a "spirit" suffuses the body . . . is there a part of it
in a part?—is there a Heaven, say, for arms?—are we eventually
rejoinable on the other side of the line the grave declares?
Well, we're still mystified by so much of the physical—why pain is 1
for patient A and 10 for patient B, or how the pink interior
roses of our flesh transmit their pleasure from the stroked skin
and the lubricating valley to a culminant expression in the brain—
that the *meta*physical is surely beyond our limited
understanding. There are nights this vicious August when Armand
—Jen's ex—will lift his eyes from his beer to watch
his endless questions on comity and abandonment and
the ciphers we are to each other ascend like smoke
from the old-time oracle fires, unraveling
in the sky, where the gods will answer them
or, likelier yet, ignore them. Back on Earth,
it's 99° for a week, and hopes and tempers blister up
like paint on sides of barns. And then a few clouds of relief
clump in; the next day, a fortissimo announcement, and the rain
falls. In the morning mist, it taps against our skin
as if another world's asking permission to enter across that line

Bright Motes in the Corner of Your Eye

His telling about the islands makes me think
of being seven, wanting changing into seventeen
and what seventeen meant of suavity and self-assurance;
at seventeen I was impatient for being thirty.
What he said was, he'd borrowed a hopper plane,
not much more than a golf cart with a propeller,
and took the islands as they came—a few days here,
a month there. Always the next one
beckoning, always bright motes in the corner of your eye.
On one, the woman had almost no hips: porpoise-hips.
On one, the woman could swear like a pirate king.
He meditated on one, in a cove, in mango light.
A storm. A goat roast. Each, its story.
Finally all of them were the same.

Toward It

Prophecy Song

And even the malls will disintegrate,
their wood to the dust of wood, their glass
to the dust of glass, their plastifoam
and diet lemonade and beveled zirconium
no more now to the wind than is the dust
of the grit of the stone of the cave at Delphi
or the slurred face of the Sphinx.
There are no two snowflakes alike—and the same
for stars of sheetrock floating out
of Victoria's Secret and The Disney Store. The flecks
of high-designer silk, the flecks of ripoff rayon,
commingle congenially as equals, even as passing storms
of globules from the transfat fryer blend now
with those inky beads of damp pressed out
from hearts of Magic 8-Balls, it will all
be chaff, and less than chaff, will all be loosened
congeries of mallecules adrift in space, yes even
Spaghetti Warehouse, even Restoration Hardware, the malls
were our temples, yet they will disintegrate
in reliable corruption as surely as Ozymandias did
and the gates of Eden. And the temples
will disintegrate. Their golden lions
or eighteen-foot-tall crosses or simple marble fonts
will go the way of the clover and the snows,
their gods will be as anise drops
in the salivations of Time—the invisible god
no less than the monkey-faced one
with the pliable, pendulous earlobes. And the holiest
of water . . . still, its hydrogen and oxygen
will each secede. The punkly, rockly, gothly, po-mo
strip club over the county line will snap
in half, and its poster announcing Hotmama Gandhi
will flash like a sorcerer's fingertips
(when dueling a fellow sorcerer with lightning beams),

and then they will settle as ash, among the ash
of the crematorium, which had a head start.
The orphanage will disintegrate, and the summer homes
of the CEO (the one in the Florida Keys, the one in the Alps)
will show the crackling of sixteenth-century Flemish art
and then disintegrate, the meth lab and the kibbutz
and the Oval Office . . . all will disintegrate,
and their people, and the-tiny-things-that-inhabit-the-grease-
of-the-eyelashes-that-those-magazines-like-*Scientific-American*-
were-always-magnifying-until-they-looked-like-Russian-tanks
of the people . . . *everything* will undo its interior mucilage,
and rise, and make its retropilgrimage back to the stars
that helio-forged the elements in the first place,
in the first time, when there was no "time," before
the solar rain of founding particles and proto-particles
fructified the barren earth, so that they could mix,
and engender further, and bring forth something
so complicated as us. That matter . . .
that energy. . . . For a while, we were its parliament,
and zodiac, and codices, and entablatures.
For a while—our while—
we were its best cohesion. For a while
we served as its likeliest integration.

"The slips for G

were very nearly burned with the
household rubbish . . ."
— Simon Winchester, on the perilous early days
of the *Oxford English Dictionary*

Germanium, geranium . . . so much
to lose! How close were we?—a glint away?
a gigabyte?—to some day seeing the gerbil
and the gnu and the giraffe and the gnat
ascend in a gyre of airborne smudge, yes
everything from garbage
to God. Everything gastrointestinal,
everything gynecological (the G-spot,
up in smoke). The goat. The gazelle.
Every grape at the greengrocer's,
every Googleable girl. The specter of imminent loss
will turn the leastmost sherd of gimcrack
into a gem. How close?—Gibraltar, Gettysburg, Genoa . . .
giving up their ghosts.

And I could spin this verbal fluff all day:
gavotte, guffaw, grisaille . . . so what?
And what about Margaret, such a tiny g in the center?
What about the cancer, such a tiny thing,
at first, in a breast? There is no g in X-ray;
none in radiation, pain, despair. And anyway
those papers toward the *OED were* saved,
if accidentally, from the fire. Their volume appeared.
Their glue was not undone, their guts weren't loosened
by nausea, they survived the grave
that waited at the end of one possibility-trail.
That was chance's gift to us.
Otherwise . . .
good-bye, good-bye.

A Word of Warning

I think it was the poet Mark Strand who
warned his fellow poets that "darkness" was
"used up," no longer a viable word for serious
writers.

— James Elkins

Easy to say so, Mr. Strand, after you've published
a book of poems called *Darker,* thus
establishing a claim
of early use, on that
impossible side of the moon.

• •

With the clumsy, creaking groan
of uncoiled machinery, and the babying touch
of archeological care, the ocean bottom is encouraged
to give up two bronze statues easily
three millennia old—three thousand years
of the full weight of the sea
on these encrusted breasts, three thousand years
without a single photon.
                    And inside, the hearts
must be like knobs of anthracite; and what they know
of love must be that kind of hole
the universe pressures into itself, where light is only
one more object,
as heavy as lead, and falling for eternity toward
an anti-place of anti-light.

• •

Well, whatever that means,
I wrote it.
       And the X-ray
of my mother's lung "revealed that she
already carried an urn of ashes
inside her." I wrote that too. I said
"my father's body fished for death
with his heart as the bait."
                  It wasn't
only dying: certain kinds of life
are an overly deep, impenetrable indigo,
they feed on the shadows under abandoned wharves
and on the unnamed stains in alleys, and I've tried to say
a thing or two for the grifters and hos
and runaway trannies and gypsy schemers
and similar rogues, whose nights play out on the farther side
of a hue we can only call "midnight." Not
that anyone understands me:
I'm the last speaker of my language.
As are you, of yours. So many words for this
one thing!—as many as people. I only know
the more you voice it,
the more you become it
. . . dark, and darker, and darkest.

The Whole of the Law of Our Human Vision

The fat tie then the thin tie then
the low hem then the to-the-coochie-hem,
it will circle around, it will all be a platter of rice cakes
filled with sweet adzuki beans on one day
then a half-pound sirloin burger under a scrimmage
of porky onion rings the next, hold parsimoniously
(or presciently or lethargically) to what was once
your favorite skinny tie because the wheel is duly bringing it
back to fashion, into a jittery,
skinny prominence again, the wheel is everything,
the universe itself is fastened (micro-quantum-mechanically)
to the wheel, it will all be the sensual snake-curls
of an architect's stencil and then the goosestep rows
of totalitarian thought, it will all be the empire rising
into ascendancy and then the estates of its gods
in ruin and then the empire rising, all the woman-space
and then the man-arena, the wheel was here before
"before" and will continue after "after," save
your fat ties, save your bowler hat and boater hat
and the derby and the deerstalker hat, oh save
the corset, the monocle, the jodhpurs, and the saris,
oh save the blood feud, save the curtsey,
the wheel is taking it all away and is returning it
(it may not be in recognizable form, but it returns),
although for us, here, in our "place" on the wheel, "here"
with our shoes and our lariats and our nipple clamps
and our Stradivarius violins that say a "time"
and finally accrue a "life," it isn't
a wheel at all, but a limited linear stretch in which
we have our pontiff vestments and our bonnets
and our bikinis and then we don't, and then we aren't,
the whole of the law of our human vision is this:
the light of an entire day,
on a cloche hat,
on a swiftly streaming river,
floating away, away.

The Bivalves Proof

Albert Goldbarth . . . this is Tom Disch . . . with a message . . .
I will not commit . . . to a machine.
— message found on my answering machine

Sometimes in the stories the visit is physical.
Odysseus even eats with the shades, he brushes against
their pliant but below-zero skin. And Orpheus:
he searches for Eurydice by passing through
the crowd down there like a cop assigned
to find an important runaway
at a race track or a concert.
Certain rabbinical mystics spent a night
in heaven watching the souls of the newly arrived
drift past—the sails of a regatta—and then
at dawn returned, a little weary, as if the journey
required stairs. Persephone: one half of the year
in Hades' grip, and one half here: an alternating current.
But for most of us, this time

among the dead is more a matter of mood
—an empathy that lingers at the corner
of Remember and Forget long past its curfew.
Some are experts—they have clambered with a weird avidity
into the opened casket of their mourning
and will not come out, will not and will not,
no bribery or psychotropic drug provides
a roadmap back. Others—dabblers; there's
the local poet, completing a series in which he imagines
his parents' deaths and then his own: a bit too Poe
manqué in key, although we surely need the poets
who remind us that we aren't haunted so much
as part of a synergy. As for me,

I've been walking around all day with my friend Tom Disch
—attached to him, almost; a system—who

abruptly left a message on my answering machine
that I never replied to, and then later that day
he killed himself. (This conversation we never had
is part of every conversation I *have* had, since;
a compound.) He was a sweet,
opinionated, and eccentrically, brilliantly verbal man.
You should try walking around with him too,
if you don't believe we're bivalves.

Disproportionate

I couldn't see into our mother's shoulder—down
its lace and its fan of vascular panpipes
to the lung, where in theory the chemo hellfire
burnt her self away with selectivity—but
setting this small sorrow against an image
of the holocaustal flames of the Nazi atrocities
seemed to clarify her smaller, individual pain,
and to give me a kind of official—at least historical—
permission to grieve. Perhaps we only understand the instant rush
of hyperventilation and amazed tears at our own,
our homespun, dramas if they're backdropped
by appropriately kindred (and yet surely

disproportionate) examples. The Valkyrian echo
and oceans-sounding, zaftig sobs of opera surrounding
your tinny tuneless humming as you enter the boss's office;
the canonically unreadable face of the Sphinx
above the unreadable face across from you at the dinner date.
Diagram the blood-links in the roll call
of ancestral presence everwebbing backward through
the gods and loves and wars of tribal history . . . and *then,* perhaps,
you'll comprehend a mother at the cribside
as she checks a dozenth time that night, and why and how
the gravitas of Shakespeare, Noh, Kabuki
is invested in her stroking of a cheek. And you might think

we'd be diminished by such contrast, we'd be one
cremated leaf in the roar of the forest fire . . . no, in fact
we're validated; now our inchling soarings-up
and sinkings have a pedigree. We *require*
the hydro-Gregorian chants of whales—Atlantic currents
as staves—or the deafening keening of chorister angels
circling by the thousands in their mourning garb, to make sense
of this photograph, this "Families identify the dead,

Crimea, 1942," with a babushka'd woman having come upon
the corpse of . . . son? or husband? stiffened in its final
brittle angles in the mud . . . her arms remembering it
from before it became an object. And this photograph,

in turn, is what we require—this shot of the two sides
of the divide—if we're going to translate into meaningfulness
this other, earlier photograph: a séance in a dim
and stately Victorian hall, where the medium's jaw is open
at its spigot, at its biochemical spigot—and as proof
of her ability to engineer a bridge to the world of the dead,
a glistering liquid ropy veil foams and pours
and hardens across her breast and onto her lap and down
to her ankles and winks in a pool there. Maybe this
outré antique depiction of the raw spot that we bear
at loss, and of—no matter how extreme—the salves we'll seek
to heal it, articulates what my sister and I would feel

at the time when the chemo failed—or, for all we knew,
collaborated eagerly with the disease—and our mother
slipped a little more each day from out of the atoms
of living as if she became a material not part of our physics.
I don't mean to underplay the part of enjoyment in this:
I've seen a child fall to, and delectate, a tomato
off the vine with such voluptuary gusto—the ultimate
smear of it over his face was like some residue of rapture—
that only the moaning from out of the sultan's pleasure palace
could hint at the distance of this transport, or
—a different metaphor—serve us as an X-ray
to illuminate his depth of experience. Also jobs:

somebody has measured, really, the weight
of a fingerprint—*a fingerprint!* Somebody sweeps
the gore away after the bullfight. (Little blood jewels.)

National Zoo biologist Sara Hollager switches the eggs
of Caribbean flamingos on Breeding Island with impressive electronic
dummy eggs, to monitor nesting (she'll return the real eggs
when they're ready to hatch): in a sense, her job
that day is to be attacked by flamingos. In a sense,
these are the visible indicia of the everyday invisible indignity
or magic of my friends in their various university cubicles
and downtown mazes of I.T. screens. My sister's job
—and this she performed with a dearly purchased surface calm—

was to telephone me with the news; I'm sure a large
and public version of her heroics exists, but I would need
to turn to those myths where fire is vomited out of the earth, or
things on leathern wings descend in the night, and somebody
faces this unassumingly. And science!—certainly. Science
as yowza correlative. The graceful coils
of ammonite fossils, from paperclip-size to tuba-!
The mind-defying theory of fourteen dimensions! Somebody
studying chimp shit under the microscope, somebody
with her eye on the light that a planet bends.
And remember the fingerprint scientist?
"Fifty micrograms is roughly the weight of a fingerprint."

No wonder the "me" of us sloughs off so quickly.

Toward It

It's good to know an aglet
is the little metal or plastic tip at the end
of a shoelace; good to know
how soil gets made; how couscous or the plastic
of a Happy Meal toy is made; and where
the G-spot really is; and how it was,
that day in 1787, when British author William Beckford
visited Madrid, and at the Monastery of San Lorenzo
was shown, or at least believed he was shown,
a feather from the Archangel Gabriel,
"lying stretched upon a quilted silken mattress . . .
three feet long, and of a blushing hue
more soft and delicate
than that of the loveliest rose." My mother's
mother's name was Rose, the cheeks they gave her
for the open-casket funeral were rose
and slightly clown-like: it was good
that her granddaughter wanted to look,
and good enough—because he knew his limits—
that her grandson declined to.

everything

On my way to Kansas City is a pond they formed
where a verdant bowl of trees once was, and the fingery tips
of the higher branches stick out . . . "like
the drowning still trying to cling to something,
even if it's the air" is how the word node
in the back of my brain attempts, each time I drive by,
to poeticize the scene . . . but in fact I remember
that Doctor Dolittle story about the Secret Lake
in the heart of "unexplored Africa" (I was eight)
with the tower tops—the spires and minarets—of a forgotten city
mysteriously poking from its surface. It's good

to remember. Some. I remember the sound
my father made in explaining his mother's death to me,
the great elk of his need to be "manly" and civil
butting head-on into the powerful locomotive
of his grief: that memory isn't "good"
in the most immediate sense; but it's instructive.
I remember . . . the little licorice strips, rolled up
to look like phonograph records . . . Dennis Madorsky's
goggle eyes and bull yell on the playground (later
he died in Vietnam) . . . the first time Claudia
undressed for me, the sweetly pink equator line
her panties-elastic left around her waist . . . it's good
to remember . . . and when we don't remember,
we remember anyway . . . it's in our heads *somehow,*
a map of faint stars in the darkness
that we migrate by, as a bird is born
with an evening sky—a hemisphere—lining its skull.

everything prepares us

The early buds, encased in a slip of late ice, so
made beautiful by what destroyed them. . . . Sun
adoring the pylons of the hydroelectric station. . . .
"FUCK YOU, ASSHOLE!". . . . The example of hundreds
of heroes in books, who didn't weep or waver
in front of the dark forbidding door. . . . A slightly
soapy scent that always seemed to accompany
the cycles of smoothing and puckering of Lillian's nipples. . . .
Everything. *Everything.* When I misheard my student June
complain of her ex's "reptile dysfunction". . . . The way
the war keeps spitting body bags out of itself as casually
as watermelon seeds. . . . The lecture on hypothermia,
making its colors as luscious as those in the throats
of prom corsages. . . . The idea that what we are

—and I mean all of us, in our human comedy-drama—
is the universe's version of neurotransmitters. . . .
Everything. In the beginning
was light; we might remember this in our under-brain
as a dim sun at the end of the vaginal tunnel. In the beginning
was a poem, it hooked me in through the soft unguarded pink
of the palate, and I've never torn free. In the beginning:
my first wife; then my second [details: see
other poems]. In the beginning: dust and breast and song.
And at the end, when sleepless pain had made itself congruent
with her body, with every aware cell of her body,
and the oncologist held no hope in his eye or pill in his hand,
my mother asked God to take her away (I didn't believe
there *was* a God, but I believed the sincerity of her prayer).
"Let Him take me away," she cried. And still, the wind
that hummed the open inch above the sill said *stay,*
the flower in the vase and the floral scent of the aerosol spray
in the bathroom and every smear of the loosening body
that colors an orderly's sponge said *stay,* and the light said *stay:*
even knowing it was impossible, the light said *stay.*
The light said *dander in me is as precious as gold.*

"How soil gets made."
"Still trying to cling to something, even if it's the air."

everything prepares us for death

[that doesn't mean we're prepared]

Practice Journey

I.

The ritzy, glitzy 24/7 exercise club—what once, in a time when neither words nor bodies were so pumped up, I would have called the "gym" and now has been termed a "mega-healthstyles emporium"—is impressive by day, on the corner here. I like especially, and I'll admit it, to look at the women (most of them so toned already, you'd think that further exercise could only be aimed at embalming those faux-tan chassis): the front of the building is almost totally glass, so that these treaders and serious huffers serve the organization as a free advertisement, even as the idea of public display is sweet to their vanity. They expose their strenuous effort and its sleeking results with obvious pride, and I (as I briskly schlep around the neighborhood for an hour—which is *my* low-rent obeisance to cardiovascular upkeep—making sure I pass this showcase building a number of times) . . . I take my part in a holistic system, and drink it all in appreciatively.

But it's really at night that the soul of the building appears. It's then that the lit front, in the midst of an otherwise dark expanse, takes on the commanding glow of a landed mothership, from some science fiction epic. And it's then, too, that the truly serious mega-health devotees appear, pumping and pounding and heave-ho lifting with such a near religious fervor, such an expert ab-by-ab near-artistry, that Michelangelo sculpting his perfected bodies out of perfect marble comes to mind . . . except that here, in their amazing conflation, these sweat-ennobled exercisers are both the sculptor *and* the torso chiseled into exquisitude.

Their arms and legs are the dream of a dream of vigor. Their hearts are dynamos. You can see in their serious frowns, and in the care of their self-study . . . they believe, or they hope, or at moments they *know:* they're going to live forever.

2.

See, the thing is, we *don't* learn from history. We barely even acknowledge it. Ours isn't a culture of husbanding and treasuring memorized lists of the ancestors dozens of generations deep. "Autobiography" entered the English language in the first decade of the nineteenth century: ever since, it's been a pell-mell immediatecentric rush from me-right-now to me-in-a-minute, and there's neither time nor room—or sensibility—for consulting the formative storage cells of the past.

The disastrous "quagmire" of Vietnam is spookily part of the human-scented smoke that floats in its heavy cover over the streets of the current "quagmire" in Iraq . . . but our eyes, though they do have vision, clearly aren't visionary, and ghosts that rise from the sands and cities of Yesteryear are no part of the wavelengths that we're wired to accept. The stupidass mistakes from the first marriage happen again— thrust and feint and snicker, parry and wail and duck—in the second and third. He may be petro-wealthier this circuit around, she may be a hotter higher-packed model, but obsolescence is built in just as surely as it was the first time, and the engine is as faulty.

"Not to know what happened before one was born is always to be a child": Cicero, about 50 B.C. We're indeed that child. "Within the wind tunnels of the high-speed electronic media, the time is always now; the data blow away or shred. . . . Not only do we lose track of our own stories (who we are, where we've been, where we might be going), but our elected representatives forget why sovereign nations go to war" (Lewis H. Lapham). Go ahead: ask my students who the Axis powers were, and who the Allies. It only requires one generation of nada transmission, and then . . . anything times zero is zero.

We don't, *don't* learn from history. Our will-to-live that has the girl with her legs blown off and her right arm severed . . . wriggling, still, with her left arm and her heaved back toward the safety of a shelter: that pulse in our plasmas *can't* afford a backward glance. The genes themselves *are* the accumulated past—but they can only point toward tomorrow.

So Dante died, and Shakespeare died, and my father now is two dates on a stone in a city—another Jewish ghetto—of dates-encumbered stone. . . . But we don't, *don't* learn from history, and my plasmas *know:* I'm not going to die. You think I will? There's no proof, and tomorrow is out there—pair of empty my-size shoes— waiting to be stepped into.

3.

My friend Dean is king of the rowing machine. Then Dean does reps, then Dean does reps, then Dean does reps. By now his body is supertrained into such a durable hardness that it looks as if, when anyone else might have stepped out from the tanning booth, he's stepped out from a kiln.

He takes, he says, 147 vitamins and homeopathic supplements a day. *A day.* (How many shapes? How many colors?) "I wouldn't have time," my friend John said, "to sort them out of the bottles, much less pop them down." Well Dean, I imagine, can readily afford an assistant to tend to the sorting, or what's a trust fund for?

The wealth, the steel thews . . . *of course* his lover is, as the other exercise fanatics have anointed her, the Goddess Amanda. Men and women both—I've seen this happen—part to allow her divinity easy passage through the outer doors and then into the workout space. The die-for face, the roseate glow, the voluminous tawny hair like a simoom about her . . . *all* of that, down to the two small arcs of museum-quality toes . . . but what particularly apotheosizes her from out of this group of exemplary specimens is that her perfect silhouette, no matter what the activity—jogging, squatting, grunting (beautifully) into the thrusts of martial arts—will never move within itself by a single errant wink or jiggle, it's so all-over firm. She sits and crosses her legs, and the upper thigh won't spread by a millimeter.

This is the drive-you-crazy part: both of them are likeable. Generous friends, charity work, modest in company, blah-blah-blah. Together, they really do look like a duo descended on cloud-steeds from Olympus, as done in the aureate schmaltz of a gods-besotted Renaissance painter. And looks and treasure aside (and what is no doubt sex-to-a-higher-power aside), they truly care for each other. I've known him to drive twenty miles out of his way to get her a rose. Once: "If I lost him, I'd die," she whispered to me.

I looked at her—how could she say that? Neither one of them was going to die.

4.

"So Dante died, and Shakespeare died. . . ." So saith Albert Goldbarth. (Surely even *our* short-term memories can call up the language in section 2.) Dickinson died, and Dickens died, and every anonymous Greek and Roman poet died, and Joanne Shmoe the performance-poet-whose-near-striptease-shenanigans-with-her-famous-slither-readings-on-open-mic-night died. . . .

The problem, for one such as me, of course is in loving them and their words, in making their wisdom a perfect secular fulfillment in the way that sacred knowledge fulfills so many others.

And dammit, one after another down the line . . . they know they're going to die, and they're casting a fishily jaundiced eye at my own denial. They somehow know that my childhood was a series of dead pet dimestore turtles, and none of them—not one—is going to let me slip around what this portends on the Goldbarthian level.

Me. Even *me?* But I'm the one who conjured up a soup restaurant to be called "The Brothel." A Jewish Oz full of "menschkins." A sundries store for Arctic explorers: "Store in a Cool Dry Place." A nude dance club: "Girls Before Swine." The universe wouldn't let *me* disappear . . . I have more of these gems, I promise! Woody Allen: "Rather than live on in the hearts and minds of my fellow man, I'd prefer to live on in my apartment."

But Keats and Chaucer and Marianne Moore and Li Po and Neruda and Whitman know that every apartment is going to be for rent again. It may be the oldest knowledge to power literature. "I sing alas for youth, alas for curst age / —the approach of one, the passing of the other." "Be young, my heart, have fun: soon other men will take / my place, and I'll be dark dust in my grave." "No return to youth / is granted by the gods to mortal men, / and no escape from death." These, anonymous lyrics from the sixth to fifth centuries BC.

Aren't I the one who's marched into class, and looked out at the pea-row under-graduate faces, and insisted to them that poetry is a mirror we hold up to see ourselves?

5.

I've broken my arm. In the middle of writing this I've slipped on the ice like any other susceptible little old man, and broken my upper right arm and set off a chain of difficult osseous complications up through the shoulder. Housebound, can't do much, so wind up looking through a drawer of old family photographs. There's my father, younger by thirty years than I am now, with the hat and pants and smile of the 1940s, there in the afternoon light of Humboldt Park. He's newly married, the smile says. The smile can't even *think* of the heart attack and the leukemia that are waiting in ambush decades later. His *own* father might well be alive still.

DEATH IS HEREDITARY, I hear myself thinking, and can't even tell if my talky subconscious has stumbled upon a profundity or burbled up another easy bumperstickerism.

And I'm reading—they're ever-fascinating—about the mummies. The ancient Babylonian dead preserved by immersion in honey. British naval hero Horatio Nelson immersed by his men, at sea, in a cask of brandy. Ancient mummies recovered from the cloud forests of the Peruvian Amazon: "Even the eyeballs and genitals are preserved." The famous wrinkled Dutch bog bodies, the webs of creases still delicate and traceable on their faces. The mummies of "incorruptible" saints in certain Italian churches, holding on to their living forms with the zealotry of Ahab holding on to Moby-Dick in death. From thirteenth century Lebanon, "a four-month-old infant, preserved down to the tiny wisps of hair between her toes"—these, likely, from the kiss of the grieving mother as she bent down. Sawing off the top of one Egyptian mummy's skull: inside, a scatter of curled-up rust-red maggots, mummified too, in the resins.

When we think of the maggots, think of the flesh flies laying their miniscule clutch of eggs in the damp of the brand-new corpse's open mouth, and what the hatchlings do as they feed their way in a pack through the muscle . . . no wonder there have been times and people dedicated to keeping the body as pure of this as possible.

And here's my father, a fossil of 1940s light on its little square. And here's my arm, on a practice journey, held still in its medical mummy wrap.

6.

Because of my arm I'm not out as much. But news like this accumulates a buzz that could work its way through a buried brick bunker. No one believes it. And still, they know, it's true. And so the buzz comes with a shock, with a resistance and yet a finality, that feel as if they have force behind them enough to someday lap, in a thinner but recognizable form, at the rims of other planets.

Dean is dead of a heart attack. It turns out the genes have a very large say in our destiny, and can't be filibustered out of their determination by a hectoring speech on fitness. At the funeral his fellow gymnauts stand around like figures on the tops of trophies, well-sculpted and eerily stiff. Is there a factory flaw invisibly somewhere in *them* too?

It turns out those ancient Greek lyrics are as contemporary as any hiphop anthem or TV cereal jingle. "I cannot prolong / my life, so why / should I cry or moan?" "The rose blooms for a brief season. It fades, / and when one looks again —the rose is a briar." "Musa the singing-girl lies here mute, / who was once so witty, so much loved." "And the old-of-death will pass their wine to the newly dead / and all will drink as equals."

Dean is dead—*Dean!* Is he sacrifice enough for a while? The rest of us—are we saved?

Hey, *I'm* the one who looked at the elastically swan-throated nudes of Modigliani's, and thought of a word for those models' deaths: neckrology. I'm working out a joke that makes sense of the punch line SQUID PRO QUO. But it will require time, a lot of time. My mind is a work in progress. *Not, not, not, not me.* Surely fate respects the rule: survival of the wittest.

Well a week chugs past, with the usual. Bills. Some half-read books. A night out with friends, maneuvering food and drink with a left-handed willingness. Students. Mail. Dreams.

And then a phone call. A spike in the buzz, that one might well have seen coming but didn't, and now what? Wordless. Now, now what? Amanda is dead of an overdose.

7.

I've broken my arm. It happens only a few months after I start my treatments for macular degeneration. They showed me the scans: there on my left eye's retinal wall was the planet Mars. I could see its lit-up orange-red tint and its polar caps and its network of canals. This meant my macula was leaking.

It's true that they numb you up well. "Do it so you could bounce a dime off the surface," I always say, and they comply. But a needle injected into your eyeball is never desirable. I've had four of those treatments now, and while they aren't guaranteed to work, they've so far created a functioning containing wall against the insidious leakage.

In a week-and-a-half I'm scheduled for my second prostate biopsy: what they call the "PSA level" was what they call "elevated" *(uh-oh)* when my annual lab work got diagnosed. I remember the first of those, five years back: they numb you up for that too, but the microcarving of microslices out of the shrieking traumatized bloody middle of you . . . is never, ever desirable.

I'm sixty, and the warranty is expired, and the rest is baby aspirin, leafy greens, and luck.

Milton was blind, and Byron was lame, and Pope was hunched and in clenches of pain every day, and Virginia Woolf combatted (sometimes with success, but sometimes yielding to its suffocations) darkness of a kind that maybe Sexton knew, Jane Kenyon knew, Sylvia Plath, and Hemingway at the end. . . .

And so? *Not me. Not me.* Woody Allen says, "I'm a firm believer that when you're dead, naming a street after you doesn't help your metabolism."

After a month, my arm gets unwrapped. The skin is a shade of whey and the muscle is atrophied. Time for physical therapy now—three times a week, as if my body *does* have a future worth suffering for, and there *are* (the weights . . . the elastic bands . . . the pulleys . . .) years of writing left. How's this:

Two squid walk into a bar. . . .

8.

He'd think they looked too thin, this man who struggled through Depression-era hunger; he'd ask if they wanted a little nosh.

So many of us (or even most, according to some polls) think it a credible scene, my father welcoming Dean and Amanda into heaven.

Not me, and not my friends. Our sense of wonder (call it "awe" or "transcendence" or "being in touch with a higher plane" or, if you want, call it "spirituality") is as great as any believer's . . . but without the supernatural involved. It's the arts that often give us access to this feeling, they really do provide the transport and the deepening of religious faith.

Without, however, an afterlife. *That's* the catch. We won't buy into the silly literality of a fairy tale, a metaphor.

And even so, our sages are here, to counsel us on days when death's demoralizing shadow slinks out of its hole and puddles across our path on its way to some engagement.

I love particularly Whitman's rousing and rhapsodic, philosophically oopy-goopy, and strategically fine-milled paean to his sense of "what's beyond," his poem "The Sleepers," in which death and sleep and night and ocean and womb and cosmic mother are so masterfully equated, are so much a part of a cyclic, recombinant process. "Why should I be afraid to trust myself to you? . . . I know not how I came of you and I know not where I go with you, but I know I came well and shall go well." There's a course I teach in which I devote twelve class-hours to the parsing of this poem.

And I teach the ancient Greek poets, so heartfelt in their adjurations to squeeze the humanistic most from the time we *do* have here—to press from it a sufficience. "Eros, put your work clothes on. / While I live, bring flowers / and my lovely mistress." "Being mortal / I cannot prolong / my life, so why / should I cry or moan? / Bring sweet wine, / bring my good friends. / I'll lie on a soft bed / and be lost in love." "I don't mourn those who are gone from the sweet light. / I mourn those who waste their sweet light in mourning."

There are undergraduate students I like, who trust me—as I trust them—in the back-and-forth of extracurricular banter. One day I notice a woman whose shorts and top reveal her knees and elbows to be rubbed pinkly raw, and I raise my eyebrows inquiringly. "Oh . . . rug burns from some sex last night."

"Ah," pipes up the voice of my subconscious, "carpet diem."

9.

The corner gym was shut for a week, a sign of elegiac respect for its two most exemplary charter members. My arm is freed from its bondage on the day the gym reopens; and that night I get to pass it again, like always, when I resume my walking. There it is: that lit cube, as if all of the strenuous exercise on display were converted immediately to the wattage that displays it. How could I *not* look, how could I *not* come close? Anybody would be a moth for this compelling engine-room of lonely illumination.

Out of all of them, tonight it's the ones on the rowing machines who hold my attention. The building appears to be theirs alone. Rowing . . . rowing . . . building up ohms . . . in unison, I could swear to that. Rowing. . . .

I stand there, shadowed away, and I watch them circle their oars through the thickness of night, with such intensity, such perseverance . . . rowing . . . .

I feel the block tug at its mooring. Then the rope is cast off. The neighborhood is moving, into the dark, to the stars, in a steady rhythm . . . rowing . . . into the unknown, into its current, into our fears and expectations.

What We Were Like (3)

"He held out his hand. 'Zarth has told me that this was the gesture of greeting in your time.'"

— Jhal Arn, Emperor of the Mid-Galactic Empire 200,000 years
in the future, to John Gordon, twentieth-century time
traveler, in Edmond Hamilton's *Return to the Stars*

In my time we shook hands.
We shook—in fear; in the sweet
depleting tremor following sex.
In my time we shook hands,
stabbed backs, held heads high,
girded loins, and gritted teeth,
we never dreamed this bodyspeech
would ever change, but that was our
presumption: nobody dances the quadrille
any longer, and few of us
play mumbletypeg. Spittoons
are scarce, and serious genuflection.
Who are we, to claim a version of eternity
for the high-five?
In my time we "gave the finger": [   ].
This was the "cuckold sign": [   ]. And this here,
making a little pare-the-apple motion in the air
alongside your temple: [   ]: "he's crazy." In my time
we were crazy; how about yours? We really thought
the oxygen and the oil and the waters had
renewal-magic written in their molecular code,
but we were wrong. Some of us wore helmets
shaped of tinfoil, to repel the brain-invasion rays
from Mars; and some of us believed the second
marriage would be effortless, we'd learned
so much from the uselessly steaming engine
of the first. We wept—presumably
you weep? You hold your head in your hands
as if you're considering bowling it down

the alley of broken hopes? Or have you
somehow evolved past bowling
and sorrow? What do you do
for laughter? Do you "hold your ribs"?
Or "slap your knees"? In my time
there was laughter, still. Its eye-rhyme
"slaughter" was plentiful, but we laughed
in the painfully godforsaken crannies.
We made "the sign of the cross," we thought
"outside of the box," and we kissed asses.
In my time there was rhyme. I made a few
of those myself. We hugged. We gave
the "rump bump" and the "knuckle bump"
and the "booty shake." That latter of course
was not indulged in by everybody.
In my time there were numerous times,
which passed in the hospital respirator ward
in ways unthought-of in the honeymoon suite
with its balcony doors agape to let
the nearby moon illumine the love
being made in a wash of sterling silver.
Maybe there were as many times as there
was us. In "my" time in my time,
as I said, I dabbled away at "poetry,"
I took my time. I brought a book of many words
to an emptiness in my heart,
and I shook them out in there, to fill it.
In my time I wrote this very thing.
In your time you read it.

Acknowledgments

All of the poems in this collection originally appeared (occasionally with small variations) in literary journals, and gratitude goes to the editors of the following:

The American Poetry Review: "The Human Condition"; Bone; Coming Back

The Believer: Whatever Surrogate

Beloit Poetry Journal: With Quotes from William Irvine's Account of the 19th Century Scientist-Explorer Thomas Huxley's Life

Boulevard: Return Suite: The Little Click; A Word of Warning

The Georgia Review: Our Heroine Ellen, and Three Pals; Miles; October; Emma (Mrs. Charles) Darwin; Struck Together; Round, Polished Stones; Perception Poem; A Partial List of Unacknowledged Musics (Feel Free to Add Your Own); Linear; Disproportionate

The Gettysburg Review: Charles's Compliment; The Versions

Hotel Amerika: The Lamps; The Story of Wax and Wane

The Iowa Review: Dynamics; Over Miles of Iowa Fields: *Snorkel, Karaoke, Leaf*

The Kenyon Review: Everyday People; Photographs of the Interiors of Dictators' Houses

The Laurel Review: "A great volume

Michigan Quarterly Review: The Winds; The Storm; That Re- (What We Are); Before Refrigeration; "A Toast!"; Toward It; Our Argument, Like the Thunderstorm,

New Letters: An Explanation; The Poem of the Dance of the Real; A Few of the Ways to Say It; The Nose in Feet; Altered; Countries

New Ohio Review: Honeycomb, Calling; Smallish; A Weather; The Whole of the Law of Our Human Vision; "He held out his hand. 'Zarth has told me that this was the gesture of greeting in your time.'"

The Paris Review: Minnows, Darters, Sturgeon

Parnassus: The Asparagus Tongs; Goth Boy: An Instruction; Unseen; Prophecy Song; "The slips for G; The Bivalves Proof

Poet Lore: Bright Motes in the Corner of Your Eye

Poetry: Natural State; The Poem of the Little House at the Corner of Misapprehension and Marvel

Prairie Schooner: STD; Ws

River Styx: That Was the Year

The Seattle Review: Practice Journey
Shenandoah: Zones
The Southern Review: Crazy Way; Off from Shore
Virginia Quarterly Review: The Poppy Fields of Afghanistan
Water-Stone: A Story
Zoland Poetry: A Typo for "Paths of Gravel" on Page 17 of Jack Williamson's *Demon Moon* (Tor Books)

"Zones" was also anthologized in *The Best American Poetry 2009* (thanks to David Wagoner). "That Re- (What We Are)" received the 2008 Laurence Goldstein Poetry Prize from *Michigan Quarterly Review* (thanks to Sandra M. Gilbert). "Our Argument, Like the Thunderstorm," received the 2011 Laurence Goldstein Poetry Prize from *Michigan Quarterly Review* (thanks to A. Van Jordan). "Practice Journey" was anthologized in the 2011 edition of the *Pushcart Prize: Best of the Small Presses* (thanks to Bill Henderson).

Seven of these poems were also collected in a limited edition hand-letterpressed chapbook, *The Neighbors,* from Scott King's Red Dragonfly Press; "Most of Us" made its initial published appearance there. "Photographs of the Interiors of Dictators' Houses," in addition to appearing in the online version of the *Kenyon Review,* was also published by that journal as a limited edition hand-printed broadside (thanks to David Lynn and Jouman Khatib).

Much of the prose in "'A great volume" is inspired by, and shamelessly uses, Rachel Carson's *The Edge of the Sea.* Research for "Practice Journey" included Heather Pringle's *The Mummy Congress*; "Preamble" in the first issue of Lewis Lapham's *Lapham's Quarterly*; inspiration from the Greek translations of Willis Barnstone, Dudley Fitts, Richard Lattimore, Kenneth Rexroth; plus, Wayne Zade helped with the Woody Allen quotes, and Skyler Lovelace and John Crisp helped with the broken arm.

Many editors have shown special kindness to me over the years. This book wants particularly to thank Herb Leibowitz at *Parnassus*; Diane Boller and Don Selby of *Poetry Daily*; and Stephen Corey (with an able assist from the infallible Mindy Wilson) for many instances of acumen and generosity on behalf of the *Georgia Review,* including—but not limited to—that journal's "Special Feature: Albert Goldbarth."

During the preparation of this manuscript David Hamilton and Laurence Goldstein announced their retirements from longstanding and invaluable editorships of, respectively, the *Iowa Review* and *Michigan Quarterly Review*; the estimable Ray Smith died, taking the *Ontario Review* with him; and Jeanne Leiby died, ending her vibrant editorship of the *Southern Review* all too early: I honor the pleasures these four have provided.

No computer was used in the creation or submission of these poems . . . and the editors of the publications I've acknowledged above, as well as the staunch and patient and open-hearted crew at Graywolf Press, have earned extra rounds of thanks for helping me continue to be me.

ALBERT GOLDBARTH has been publishing books of note for forty years, including *The Kitchen Sink: New and Selected Poems 1972–2007,* which was a finalist for the *Los Angeles Times* Book Prize and received the Binghamton University Milt Kessler Award. Among other honors, he has twice won the National Book Critics Circle Award in poetry, and has received a Guggenheim Fellowship, three fellowships from the National Endowment for the Arts, and the Poetry Foundation's Mark Twain Award. In addition to his poetry, Goldbarth is the author of five collections of essays, including *Many Circles: New and Selected Essays,* and a novel, *Pieces of Payne.* He lives in Wichita, Kansas.

Everyday People has been set in Adobe Garamond Pro, a typeface drawn by Robert Slimbach and based on type cut by Claude Garamond in the sixteenth century. Book design by Ann Sudmeier. Composition by BookMobile Design and Publishing Services, Minneapolis, Minnesota. Manufactured by Versa Press on acid-free 30 percent postconsumer wastepaper.